Hannibal And The Great War Between Rome And Carthage

Walter Wybergh How

HANNIBAL

AND THE

GREAT WAR BETWEEN ROME AND CARTHAGE

BY

W. W. HOW, M.A.

Fellow and Tutor of Merton College, Oxford

LONDON
SEELEY AND CO. LIMITED
38 GREAT RUSSELL STREET
1899

PREFACE

IN writing this short life of Hannibal, I have endeavoured to meet
the needs of intelligent boys in the upper forms of schools, but I
hope that it may also be acceptable to older readers unafflicted by
the dread of examinations. The story is one which will bear re-
telling, often as it has been already told. I have throughout based
my account on the chief ancient authorities, Polybius and Livy,
though want of space has forbidden detailed quotation from their
works. Neither historian does entire justice to the greatness of
Hannibal; for Polybius, with every intention to be impartial, was
too much under the influence of the Scipionic family traditions, and
too cold by temper to feel the full nobility of the Carthaginian
leader; and Livy, a patriot by profession and a slanderer in practice,
totally misunderstood and misrepresented Rome's greatest enemy.
Yet Polybius is a sound historian, if a dull writer, and Livy a
vivid and picturesque writer, if a careless and untrustworthy
historian. Little of value is to be found in the pages of the other
ancient authors who have touched more briefly on the career of
Hannibal.

In modern times a long array of historians biographers and
commentators have expended much learning and ingenuity on this
fascinating subject. Among the historians of Rome I owe most to
Professor Mommsen, who has drawn with a master's hand the
character and institutions of the two rival powers, and has best
summed up the political and military lessons of the struggle between
them, and to Dr Arnold, whose brilliant and sympathetic description
of the Second Punic War has been enriched with valuable notes by

his grandson. On Carthaginian history I have consulted Dr Meltzer's *Geschichte der Karthager*, so far as it goes, and Mr Bosworth Smith's *Carthage and the Carthaginians*.

Three recent biographies of Hannibal deserve special mention. Colonel Hénnébert's learned and exhaustive treatise labours under two defects—a rather uncritical use of the authorities, and a lack of proportion between the different parts of the work—yet it remains a monument of patient industry. Colonel Dodge's careful and able description of the organisation and operations of the Roman and Punic armies has been of great assistance to me; in my estimate of Hannibal's genius for war I owe much to his luminous criticisms, as well as to the interesting popular biography by Mr O'Connor Morris. For the plans of Cannæ and of the Trebia I am indebted to the delegates of the Clarendon Press; that of Lake Trasimene I owe to Mr Grundy. By a visit to the site I have been led to accept in the main his view of that battle, while on Cannæ I follow Mr Strachan-Davidson. In conclusion, I must acknowledge my deep obligation to my friends, Mr Henderson and Mr Leigh. The former allowed me to read the manuscript of his critical papers on the Campaign of the Metaurus (published in the *English Historical Review*, 1898), and drew my attention to several German and Italian articles there quoted, in particular to the ingenious researches of Bossi. The latter permitted me to draw freely on his account of Hannibal in our history of Rome, and added to his kindness by reading the present work in manuscript and making many valuable suggestions.

WALTER W. HOW.

OXFORD, *January* 18, 1899.

CONTENTS

PLANS

HANNIBAL

CHAPTER I

CARTHAGE AND ROME

THE Carthaginians were sprung from the Phœnician branch of the Semitic stock. Their forefathers had dwelt in the land of Canaan, and even
in its African home the people still called itself
Canaanite. On the narrow strip of plain which
borders the Syrian highlands, the Phœnicians had
built themselves great cities—Tyre and Sidon,
Byblus and Aradus. The country was fertile if
small, but an abundant supply of timber from
Mount Lebanon, and the excellence of their harbours, naturally led the Phœnicians to pass beyond
the limits of their own land and embark on the
widespread waters of the Mediterranean. From
the dawn of history this enterprising race devoted
its best energies to the development of commerce,
of navigation and of colonisation. Like the Genoese
in mediæval times, or the English to-day, the

A

Phœnicians were the great carriers of the world. Through their hands passed the ivory and slaves of Africa, the gold and pearls of the East, the linen of Egypt, the spices of Arabia, copper from Cyprus, iron from Elba, Cornish tin and Spanish silver. They covered the lands with a network of caravan routes, and girdled the Mediterranean with factories on every shore. But while they were thus everywhere the porters of material civilisation, of its spiritual gifts and graces they were singularly devoid. In art and science they had not the creative originality of the Chaldee and of the Hellene : in faith and morals they lacked the high ideals which have made the prophets of Israel the teachers of the world. They spoke a language akin to the Hebrew, yet they created no literature like that of the Old Testament. Their extant inscriptions are uninteresting and monotonous, and their supposed invention, the alphabet, turns out to be a commercial adaptation of signs and syllabaries already current on the coast lands of the Mediterranean. Here, as elsewhere, the Phœnicians borrowed freely from the higher civilisations established on the banks of the Nile and Euphrates, or on the shores of the Ægean, and turned their stolen goods to the best financial account. Again, though their municipal organisation was in form similar to the city-state of classical antiquity, the men of Tyre and Sidon had not the political instinct or the power of assimilating lower races possessed by the Hellene and the Italian.

Hence the Phœnicians sacrificed ideals on the altar of material interests. They successively surrendered their liberty to Egyptian and Assyrian kings in order to preserve their hold on the trade of the East and of Africa. They allowed themselves to be gradually supplanted in the Levant by their Greek rivals. But when pursued by those rivals to the Western Mediterranean, even Phœnician patience turned to bay, as Tyre had turned upon the Assyrian, and was yet to turn upon Alexander. Such was the origin of that long struggle between Semite and Aryan for the possession of Sicily, the key of the West, which is the central fact in the history of that island in ancient as in mediæval times.

In this new policy of resistance to the encroach- Carthage. ments of Hellenic emigrants, Carthage was the champion of the Semitic race. The advantages of its situation and the energy of its people enabled it soon to outstrip in power and wealth not only its elder sister Utica, but even the mother city Tyre. Built on the fertile slopes of the bay of Tunis, commanding the best harbour in the gulf, Carthage naturally took the lead in agriculture, in commerce and in manufactures. The old town itself, with its citadel Byrsa and circular harbour Cothon, was protected by a triple line of stupendous fortifications ; even the pleasant spreading suburbs Megara were surrounded by a wall, slighter indeed, but amply sufficient to repel attack. Thus strong in wealth and secure within her mighty walls, Carthage could afford to exchange the old policy of submission and self-effacement for a new imperial policy of resistance and conquest. It was indeed time for the Semites to bestir themselves. Western Sicily was now dominated by Selinus and Acragas, Southern Gaul by Massilia, while in Africa itself Cyrene was a formidable rival.

Carthage proved herself equal to the task imposed on her. She set a limit to the advance of Cyrene; by her defence of Motye and Panormus against the assaults of the Greeks, she fastened her grip on Western Sicily; she assisted the Etruscans to repel the Hellenic invaders from their coasts.

Carthaginian Empire in Africa.

At the same period Carthage built up an empire in Libya. The other Phœnician settlements became dependent on the great imperial city. The native farmers were reduced to the position of fellaheen, while the nomad tribes of the desert willingly or unwillingly obeyed her commands. Thus in this African empire there were, besides the native Carthaginians, three classes of subjects. The Liby-Phœnicians were the inhabitants of the towns founded by Carthage or by the mother-cities of Tyre and Sidon, which acknowledged the hegemony of Carthage and fought under her banner. Like the Latins in the earlier days of Rome, the Liby-Phœnicians lived under the same laws as the Carthaginians, in that they could buy and sell, inherit and bequeath property, and contract marriages with them on equal terms. Yet, politically, Leptis, Hippo, Thapsus and the other cities were, like the states of the Athenian empire, rather subjects than allies. They had to provide contingents for the army and to pay tribute. Only Utica retained a nominal independence and equality. Carthage absorbed the foreign trade and furnished the navy.

The Libyans were an agricultural population reduced to practical serfdom by Carthaginian capitalists. They were subject to tribute, to trade restrictions and to a regular system of recruiting for the Carthaginian army. Constantly irritated by the insolence of individuals or the harshness of a suspicious and arbitrary government, the Libyans were a standing menace to Carthage. Nor were the Numidian tribes who retained the pastoral roving habits of their forefathers more trustworthy. Loyal to their own sheiks, the horsemen of the desert were impatient of foreign domination. They would follow a prince like Syphax or Massinissa, or a captain like Hannibal to the death, but their tempers were uncertain and their allegiance unstable.

Outside Africa the Carthaginian empire included Malta and Western Sicily, the fringe of Sardinia and Corsica, the southern coast of Spain, and the Colonial Dominion of Carthage.

Baliaric Isles. Sardinia was organised like Libya,
the agricultural population being exploited for the
benefit of the Phœnician colonists on its coasts.
Spain was highly valued for its mines, Sicily for
its fertile corn land and spacious harbours. The
island was won and lost again and again, but
Carthage at length triumphed over the Greek, only
to fall before the Roman. Speaking generally,
the organisation of the foreign empire was dictated
by the spirit of commercial monopoly, rather
than by the true interest of the subjects or the
necessities of military defence. The empire
depended for its very existence on the maintenance of maritime supremacy and the command
of the sea.

Home
Govern-
ment. The outline of the Carthaginian constitution is
well known to us, though its details are obscured
by the contradictions and omissions in the ancient
authorities. As in Greece Rome and Phœnicia,
monarchy had been gradually superseded by republican institutions of a municipal type. The
spirit that animated the government was distinctly
oligarchic. A few noble and wealthy houses
monopolised office and power, leaving to the
ordinary citizens only the shadow of liberty. The
chief magistrates were the two annual Shofetes or
judges, who retained of their ancient royal prero-
gatives little but the presidency of the Senate and
the right of jurisdiction. Far greater were the
ill-defined powers of the general in the field.

Like the Roman dictator, he was a temporary monarch; unlike him, he enjoyed his powers for an indefinite time. The general was hampered no doubt by the presence of senators in his camp, and had to face on his return the strict scrutiny of a jealous government, but more than once this monarchy abroad threatened to be too strong for the oligarchy at home. The characteristic organs of the home government were the Senate or Gerousia, and the body of one hundred and four judges. Both would seem to have been in a sense committees of a large council, which represented the whole class of Punic nobles, as the *Maggior Consiglio* represented the nobility of Venice. But this unwieldy council had no real influence on affairs. The Senate chosen annually by the citizens from the nobles took into its hands the entire administration of the state. It managed finance, it despatched embassies, it levied armies and named their generals. But behind and above this Senate, like the mysterious ten at Venice, stood the hundred and four judges.

Like the Ephors at Sparta, this body formed no part of the original constitution, and like them it developed powers originally judicial into a general right of supervision. Its members were chosen every year, but in practice retained their office for long periods. Thus the board of judges became a close corporation, constituted by co-optation summoning generals and Shofetes to give account of their stewardship, controlling even the Senate. It was the keystone of an oligarchic constitution, whose foundations were wealth and noble birth.

The people at Carthage, the petty traders artizans and seamen, had few political rights or privileges. When the Shofetes and Senate could not agree, questions of policy and legislative proposals came before the assembly. The nomination of generals and Shofetes by the Senate was ratified by the voice of the multitude. But the city populace was corrupt and fickle, and though filled with the love of hearth and home, it afforded no firm foundation for the reforms of the patriotic party led by Hannibal. Wealth remained the dominant power at Carthage, and this oligarchy of commerce, while it often displayed prudence and moderation, never could rise above the narrow exclusiveness and the jealous suspicions of a great trading company.

Comparison between Carthage and Rome.

Let us now compare the resources and strength of Carthage with those of her great rival Rome. Both alike were flourishing cities, prominent in commerce and in agriculture, but in Carthage the monied interest was stronger than the landed; in Rome, the yeomen still formed the mass of the burgesses. In Carthage there was an opulent nobility and a landless populace, in Rome, rulers and ruled alike had as yet a stake in the country.

(1) In Constitution. In their constitutions again there was much apparent similarity. Both

were in form mixed constitutions, in spirit aristocratic. But the Carthaginian Senate and judges
mistrusted both the populace they governed and
the magistrates who should have been their leaders ;
the Roman Senate, which during the Punic wars
represented the nation, could trust the people
and dreaded no usurpation on the part of the
magistrates. Thus the solid Roman state carried
through a firm policy, and never shrank from
the greatest dangers ; the Carthaginian, a house
divided against itself, was easily elated by prosperity and cast down by misfortunes.

(2) In the organisation of their dominions.
Still more vital is the difference in the organisation of their dominions. Rome was the head of
an Italian confederacy whose territory was con-
pact, and bound to the capital by a network
of roads and fortresses. Within this national
unity under her supremacy, Rome allowed a large
measure of local liberty. Each city might manage
its own internal affairs, but must follow the lead of
Rome in foreign policy. For the maintenance of
her suzerainty, Rome employed two effective instru-
ments—isolation and gradation of privilege. Each
city was separated from its neighbours by the
dissolution of the old tribal leagues, and linked to
Rome by special favours or hope of promotion.
At the head of the Italian league stood the full
citizens of Rome, resident either in the neighbourhood of Rome or in the lands assigned to them

from the confiscated territory in Italy, especially in
the burgess colonies. Beneath them came citizens
in townships (*municipia*), with various degrees of
local autonomy, who were all subject to the war-
tax (*tributum*) and service in the legions, and possessed the private rights of Roman burgesses.

Over against these two classes of full and half
citizens stood the allied states, bound to equip and
pay a contingent of troops or ships and crews, but
enjoying full local autonomy and exempt from taxation. Foremost among them were the colonies
of Latin right, which possessed more independence than a burgess colony, and ampler rights than
ordinary allies. On the firm barrier of these Latin
fortresses the waves of Hannibal's invasion were
to beat in vain, for their citizens, who owed all to
Rome, were faithful to her cause in weal or woe·
But even the inferior allies were bound to their
suzerain by solid benefits and ties of sentiment.
The enjoyment of peace and freedom, which
implied unfettered jurisdiction and exemption
from taxation, a share in the fruits of victory, and
in the prestige of the Roman name, with the hope
of the full attainment of Roman citizenship in
the future, these were the boons conferred on Italy
by Rome. A common hatred for the Canaanite
united Greek and Italian in opposition to Hannibal.
The Carthaginian dominions, on the other hand,
were loosely organised, and fell to pieces as soon
as a hostile army, under an Agathocles or a Regu-

lus, set foot on African soil. Even the Phœnician cities had to bear the burden of tribute without receiving a share in the profits of the empire. The native races, whether subject Libyans or free Numidians, were not linked to Carthage by any bond of interest or affection. Thus, while the Roman alliance was as firm as a chain of adamant, the Carthaginian was as fragile as a web of gossamer.

In finance Carthage, the London of antiquity, had a great advantage. Its revenues so far excelled those of other city-states as to be compared by Greek authors to those of the Persian king. Carthage had anticipated modern financiers by inventing a token-money and foreign loans. But the sources of the Punic revenue—tribute and customs—were apt to fail just when they were most needed under stress of war.

(3) In military and naval power. The military strength of the two great Western powers was not unequal, but so different in character as to baffle comparison. Rome depended on the splendid fighting qualities of the Italian farmers. The total force liable to service in the field may have numbered some 700,000 footmen and 70,000 horse, of whom rather more than a third were Roman citizens. In ordinary times the consuls annually levied and discharged a force of four legions, to which the Roman citizens contributed some 16,800 infantry and 1200 horse, the allies 20,000 foot and

3600 horse, but in the war with Hannibal the number of legions rises above twenty. Before the Punic wars, the open manipular order of battle had superseded the old solid phalanx. The legionaries were formed in three divisions, the younger men (*hastati*), 1200 strong, in front, the men in their prime, also 1200 in number, in the second line (*principes*), and in reserve the 600 veterans (*triarii*). Each division was broken up into ten maniples or companies, which were arrayed sometimes in continuous lines, sometimes with intervals between the companies, like the squares on a chessboard. Every legionary wore a bronze helmet, a cuirass and greaves, and carried a large oblong shield. Their offensive weapons varied at different times. The short stabbing Spanish sword was adopted during the second Punic war. At the same period the two front divisions were armed with the *pilum*, an iron-pointed wooden javelin, six feet and a half in length, which could be hurled by practised hands with force and precision. The veterans alone now used the old thrusting spear. Thus the legion opened the battle with the discharge of missiles from a distance, and followed up their volleys of javelins by charging home, sword in hand.

But if the Roman infantry was a model for all time, in cavalry and auxiliary forces the army was weak. The old irregular skirmishers (*rorarii*)

proved utterly useless, and had to be superseded
(211 B.C.) by a new corps of *velites*, who also served
to strengthen the cavalry. The cavalry, few in
numbers, badly armed and badly handled, proved
a dangerous source of weakness in the Roman
army. The need of auxiliary forces such as
archers and slingers was forced on the notice of
Rome during the struggle with Hannibal.

The Carthaginian army was in sharp contrast
with the Roman both in its merits and defects.
Its weakness lay in the want of a patriotic and
trustworthy infantry. In early days many thousands of citizens had taken their place in the ranks
of the hosts that invaded Sicily, but by 300 B.C.
the burgess troops had dwindled down to a sacred
band 2000 strong, who formed the bodyguard of
the general, and in the armies of Hamilcar and of
Hannibal the Carthaginians only served as officers.
The burgess-militia, some 40,000 strong, was not
called out unless an enemy landed in Africa, and
had not the steadiness and discipline of regular
troops. The kernel of the Punic army was formed
from the Libyans, but the native levies, had to be
supplemented by a motley host of mercenaries.
The best among them were the Iberian heavy
cavalry and infantry, but there were also found
in the ranks small but hardy Ligurians, and huge
unwieldy Gauls. Neither mercenaries nor subjects
lacked bravery or skill in arms, but the ties which
bound together Punic armies—military obedience

and selfish interest—were weak when tried against the patriotism of the Italians.

But if Carthage was inferior in infantry of the line, she excelled in the number and variety of her auxiliary forces. The Numidians supplied the best light cavalry in the world; the Spanish and Gallic heavy horse and the Baliaric slingers more than once inclined the scale of victory in favour of Carthage. Lastly, in material of war Carthage was superior. Her arsenals were full of military machines and stores, the stables in her casemates held 300 elephants.

On the sea Carthage had once reigned in un-questioned supremacy. After the defeat of Syra-cuse, no power attempted to contest with the Phœnician the empire of the Western Mediter-ranean. Rome was hopelessly inferior in the build of her ships and in the skill of her seamen. But in the first Punic war her iron constancy had triumphed over all difficulties. Quinqueremes were built, we are told, on the model of a stranded Carthaginian ship; the superior manœuvring and tactics of the Punic fleet were neutralised by the invention of the boarding-bridge (*corvus*), which enabled Duilius to fight a land battle on the sea; the way to Africa was opened by the battle of Ecnomus, and in spite of the defeat of Regulus and the heroic struggles of Hamilcar, the victory of Rome was assured by the destruction of the Carthaginian fleet off the Ægatian Islands. That decisive battle not only compelled Carthage to surrender Sicily, but deprived her of that complete command of the sea on which her empire, and even her existence, depended. It was plain that the war for Sicily was but the first stage in the great struggle between Rome and Carthage, and that the duel must be fought out in Italy or in Africa. But while an invasion of Italy by a Punic army was but the beginning of a long war, a Roman landing in Africa was likely to be its end. In spite of the defects in the Roman system—the annual election of two inexperienced generals and the division of the command between them—the patriotism of her citizen soldiers, the loyalty of her allies, and the wise tenacity of the Senate, gave Rome a great advantage over her rival. Neither colossal wealth nor sea power could save Carthage from inevitable subjection. There yet remained the chance that the military and political genius of an individual might redress the uneven balance and redeem the errors and shortcomings of a nation.

CHAPTER II

HAMILCAR AND HANNIBAL

The Barcids.

AT the end of the first Punic war, Carthage appeared to be at the mercy of Rome. She had lost Sicily, and what was far worse, her commercial monopoly and her command of the sea; she still possessed Africa, the Spanish trading stations and the gates of the Atlantic. But her tenure even of Africa was precarious, now that Rome from Lilybæum commanded the passage between the Eastern and Western portions of the Mediterranean. Such an existence by the grace of Rome was unworthy of a great nation. It was the mission of the family of the Barcids to avert for a time the impending ruin of Carthage; to fire the people with their own ardent patriotism, to shame even the selfish aristocracy into a show of action, and at last, in the person of Hannibal, to humble the pride of Rome to the dust, and destroy for ages the prosperity of the Italian people.

Hamilcar.

The first of this family of heroes was Hamilcar Barca, the only great general in the first Punic war. Almost alone, without aid from Carthage, he had maintained the war in Sicily for six long years. From the impregnable hill of Ercte (Monte Pellegrino) for a time he threatened Panormus, and later established himself on Mount Eryx, above Drepana, where he held a difficult position between the Roman army, which lay before the town, and the garrison, which occupied the temple at the top of the mountain. Here by a war of outposts and surprises he schooled and disciplined his troops, and by his daring and success attached his fickle mercenaries to himself. But the destruction of the last Punic fleet off the Ægatian Isles made the surrender of Sicily inevitable. Hamilcar, himself unconquered, must deliver up to the victorious Roman his mountain stronghold, and the virgin fortresses Lilybæum and Drepana, which for three centuries had resisted every assault of their enemies (241 B.C.). He retired with all the honours of the war, filled with undying hatred for the conquerors.

On his return to Africa, Hamilcar found his native country on the brink of utter ruin. He had been unable to pay his mercenaries during the last years of the war, and had vainly petitioned the government to give him the necessary money. Compelled to send his men to be paid off in Africa, he had prudently divided them into small detachments. But the home government waited till the whole force was gathered together near Carthage, and then attempted to reduce the rate

The Mercenary War.

B

of pay. Naturally a mutiny broke out among the cheated and discontented troops, under the leadership of Spendius, a Campanian, Matho, a Libyan, and Autaritus, a Gaul. The Libyan subjects, burning to avenge the proscriptions and confiscations which had punished their real or supposed complicity with Regulus, rose in revolt, and the military mutiny became a general revolution of merciless ferocity, known as the truceless war. The incapacity of Hanno, the leader of the oligarchy, endangered the very existence of Carthage. The city was besieged on two sides, and the army which took the field routed by the insurgents. At length, in dire distress, the government besought the heroic Hamilcar to save it from the penalty of its criminal folly. But even in this extremity the oligarchs joined his discredited rival, Hanno, with him in the command of the indignant army. Hamilcar used his influence with the Numidian chiefs and the revolted cities to isolate the mutineers, and proved his military genius by speedily stamping out the rebellion.

Action of Rome.

To crown her misfortunes, Carthage had now to fear another war with Rome. The Senate had indeed refused, for very shame, to make common cause with the rebels; it, had allowed Hiero of Syracuse to assist the hard-pressed city with men and money, it had even permitted the Carthaginians to levy recruits in Italy, and had forbidden Italian traders to deal with the insurgents. But this formal recognition of treaty obligations did not prevent the Senate from procuring the release of Italian merchantmen, who had transgressed the order and fallen into the hands of Hamilcar, nor discourage the insurgents from appealing to Rome for aid. The Senate had the firmness to reject the overtures of Utica, but when the Sardinian mutineers, hard pressed by the mountain tribes of the interior, offered the island to Rome, the temptation to accept so rich a gift was too strong. With characteristic hypocrisy, Rome justified this act of brigandage by the plea that Sardinia was now an ownerless property. Naturally, however, when Hamilcar had brought back Africa to her allegiance, the Carthaginians sent an embassy to Rome to claim the restitution of the island. The Romans replied with frivolous countercharges, and ended the discussion by declaring war. But Carthage, exhausted by the long struggle with Rome, and all but ruined by the civil war whose embers were hardly now extinct, was in no condition to undertake another conflict. She was summoned to cede Corsica as well as Sardinia, and to pay an indemnity of 1200 talents (238 B.C.).

No course was left to the patriotic party but instant submission. The hope of vengeance for highhanded injustice lay deep in their hearts, but they hardly knew how to prepare for the future duel with the insolent aggressor. Their first step was to secure a firm position for their great leader

Parties at Carthage.

Hamilcar. To overthrow the governing oligarchy, rotten as it was, would have shaken Carthage to its foundations, and might have precipitated the conflict with Rome, but power, if not office, was a necessity. Hamilcar, the saviour of his country, had been rewarded·with impeachment by the oligarchic faction, who tried to throw on him the blame for the mercenaries' mutiny. The popular leader needed a position independent of the home government, beyond the reach of the jealous and envious nobility. He was appointed commander-in-chief by the vote of the popular assembly, by which alone he could be recalled and tried for his acts. Thus the control of the army and the direction of the foreign policy passed into the hands of the great patriot and statesman; the Romanising grandees were content to enjoy undisturbed the honours and profits of office.

Hamilcar in Spain. After the conclusion of the Mercenary war, Hamilcar at once restored order in Numidia. Then he marched westwards along the coast, accompanied by his son-in-law Hasdrubal at the head of a fleet, and crossed to Spain in the summer of 237 or 236 B.C. Before he left Carthage, Hamilcar had called his young son Hannibal to his side as he stood by the altar of Baal, and asked him if he too would like to go. With childish eagerness the boy caught at his father's offer. Then Hamilcar bade him lay his hand upon the victim and swear never to be the friend of Rome. Hannibal took the oath, and never to his last hour forgot his high calling. For indeed this oath embodies the solemn purpose which pervaded the lives of both father and son. Hamilcar went to Spain, to find there a 'new world to redress the balance of the old,' and in that distant land to forge the weapons of vengeance for the wrongs of Carthage. But for long years the kingly statesman and general must possess his soul in patience. He had to create an army from the Libyan conscripts and Spanish tribesmen, he had to make the war support the war, and he must even find in Spain resources from which to supply his friends at home with bribes for the venal rabble of Carthage. To gain time for the conquest of Spain he must allay the suspicions of his enemies abroad and at home. To the Roman and Punic Senates he must pretend that he sought in Spain compensation for the lost revenues of Sicily and Sardinia, and the means of paying the indemnity to Rome. These varied tasks Hamilcar accomplished with complete success. On the basis of a few trading stations held by Carthage in Southern Spain he founded a mighty kingdom. Tartessus had long been the Eldorado of antiquity, but hitherto Carthage had possessed only a few factories in Andalusia and a protectorate over the old Phœnician port of Gades. As Clive and Warren Hastings in the East Indies made of a mere trading company an imperial power, so the Barcids gradually won for Carthage the most fertile lands and the richest mines in Iberia. The fierce tribesmen were trained to fight in the Punic army, they found a home in the camp, and a form of patriotism in deep and faithful devotion to their royal-hearted leader.

Hasdrubal. For nine years Hamilcar toiled untiringly at his great work in Spain, and when he fell in battle with an Iberian tribe, he left his grand designs to the care of his son-in-law and successor Hasdrubal. (229-8 B.C.). The new governor extended the Spanish realm rather by diplomacy than by arms. The fairest and richest regions became Phœnician provinces, and the only good harbour on the south-eastern coast was chosen for the capital of the country. New Carthage (Cartagena) was dominated by the splendid castle of its founder Hasdrubal. The Spanish chiefs were won over by every device of a skilful policy, conscripts were levied in the subject territory, and mercenaries hired from the allied tribes. The new dependency became a great market for Carthaginian goods, and furnished Africa with metals, and above all with silver from Cartagena and copper from the Sierra Morena. Even the oligarchs at home were led to approve of the Barcid rule in Spain by the manifest benefits it conferred on Carthage.

Roman Inaction. The reasons for Rome's inaction are more complicated. The Senate went so far as to dispatch a commission to demand explanations, and can hardly have been deceived by Hamilcar's answer that his object in conquering Spain was to provide money for the war indemnity due to Rome. But the Roman government did not understand the wealth and resources of the remote peninsula, nor imagine for a moment that an invasion of Italy from Spain was within the bounds of possibility. It hoped that the projects of Hamilcar would perish with their author, and when that hope failed, it was too fully occupied in the conquest and organisation of Cisalpine Gaul to intervene with effect. Yet even under the pressure of the Gallic war, Rome strove to set limits to the Punic power in Spain. In 226 B.C., a Roman embassy warned Hasdrubal to respect the boundary of the Ebro, and attempted to raise up a Roman faction by offers of support to Emporiæ and Saguntum. Hasdrubal, who was rather a diplomatist than a soldier, promised compliance with the demands of Rome, regarding the recognition of the Barcid rule in Spain as of greater importance than the attempt to limit its growth by a paper boundary. Neither side was yet prepared for war. Rome wanted time to complete the conquest of the Celts in the plain of the Po, and Hasdrubal had not yet consolidated his newly won dominion. The Senate was fully convinced that the next war with Carthage would be fought in Spain and Africa, and was well content to have secured a base from which the Punic provinces in Spain might be attacked and conquered. It could not

conceive that its defeated foes were meditating a
fatal blow at the heart of Rome. But the period
of doubt and hesitation was soon to end. In 221
B.C. Hasdrubal fell by the hand of an assassin, and
Hannibal was called by the voice of the army and
of the people to fill his place.

Hannibal.   In him Carthage at last found a leader able to
use the weapon Hamilcar had forged, to throw the
might of Spain into the scale, and once more meet
Rome on even terms.

The army of Spain had been trained by long
years of fighting, and was now ready to face the
Roman infantry in the field ; the exchequer was
full ; the government was swayed by the patriotic
party ; the nation was ready to support its leader
in the inevitable conflict. To this war of vengeance Hannibal had been dedicated from his boy-
hood. Trained to arms under his father's eye, he
had early learned to bear with cheerfulness the
want of sleep or food. Brought up in the camp,
he became a hardy athlete and fearless horseman,
but he was not without the elements of culture.
After Hamilcar's death, the young man became
the chief lieutenant of Hasdrubal, and proved himself a brilliant cavalry officer. When called to the
supreme command, he, though but twenty-five years
of age, was more than worthy of his comrades'
choice. He was filled with a double measure
of his father's spirit, and, true heir of his hate and
of his genius, he was the moving and directing

power in that great storm of war which from North and South, from West and East, broke on the hapless land of Italy. Like Napoleon, he undertook to measure his strength against the stable institutions and limitless resources of a free and mighty people. In each case national tenacity triumphed over individual genius, but never were men better equipped for the struggle than were Napoleon and Hannibal. As a general, Hannibal combined the most opposite merits. At one moment bold to the verge of rashness, at another patient almost beyond the limits of caution, he never failed to adapt his plans to the character of his opponents, and to take full advantage of their faults and foibles. Equally at home in the widest problems of strategy and in the minutest questions of tactics and armaments, he proved himself a past master of the art of war in all its branches. In three points he excelled all other generals—in the unequalled control he maintained through good and evil fortune over an army composed of diverse nations speaking many tongues; in the power of divining as it were by instinct the plans of his enemies, and turning to his own advantage the varieties of their character and abilities; and in a peculiarly Phœnician subtlety which made him delight in ambushes stratagems and surprises. His gifts as a statesman and a diplomatist are proved by his wide-reaching alliances against Rome, and by his well-considered schemes of reform at Carthage. Nor was his character unworthy of his abilities. Rome indeed charged him with perfidy and cruelty, and Carthage complained of his avarice. But his avarice, if such it can be called, was simply the imperious need of a general who through long years must maintain himself in a hostile land; his perfidy and cruelty rest on the unjust accusations of his ungenerous conquerors. Now and again his lieutenants Mago and Hannibal Monomachus were guilty of savage deeds done in his name—once after Trasimene a capitulation granted by Maharbal is repudiated by Hannibal himself—but for the most part the charges which have blackened the name of Hannibal are but calumnies prompted by malice and envy. His supposed perfidies are often legitimate stratagems which deceived the inexperience and stupidity of Roman generals; his cruelties the stern but necessary exertion of rights sanctioned by the usage of the day. And through all the clouds of misrepresentation there stands out a pure and noble image of a character distinguished by chivalrous generosity towards fallen enemies, and unshaken fortitude in adversity.

Hannibal in Spain.
To Hannibal, war with Rome was not a question of national aggrandisement, still less was it dictated by personal ambition or the hope of founding a dynasty; it was a patriotic duty, a charge bequeathed to him by his father, the only path of honour and of safety for his country. Yet

he did not rashly force on the tremendous struggle. He spent the first two years of his command in the conquest of the tribes holding the central plateau of Spain, the Olcades the Vaccaei and the Carpetani. In the course of these campaigns Hannibal gave a striking proof of his mastery in the art of war. While he had been employed in subduing the Vaccaei, two tribes rose behind him and took up a commanding position near Toledo, at a ford on the Tagus. They thought to force battle on an army laden with spoil, and overwhelm it with superior numbers. Hannibal, when he found himself attacked, merely repulsed the barbarians and occupied a strong defensive position. But when night fell he broke up his camp, crossed the river by another ford, and at daybreak had posted himself on the further bank opposite the ford held by the Spaniards. The barbarians, ascribing his manœuvre to fear, rushed pell-mell across the stream to overwhelm him. But Hannibal had so laid his plans as to ensure their destruction. Along the banks he posted his footmen and elephants, and in the centre opposite the ford his cavalry. As the Spaniards thronged into the river, the Punic horse charged them and rode them down in mid-stream, while the elephants trampled upon and the footmen cut to pieces those who struggled to the bank. Finally, recalling his horse, Hannibal sent his infantry in column across the ford to smite the disordered masses of the enemy. Before their charge the barbarians fled in confusion, hotly pursued by the Carthaginian cavalry. By this feat of arms Hannibal inspired both the army and the home government with confidence, and established his authority in Spain from Cape St Vincent to the Ebro.

Saguntum. Then an occasion of war was found in the ambiguous position and attitude of Saguntum. The town, which lay far south of the Ebro, within the boundaries of the Punic dominions, claimed nevertheless to be under the protection of Rome.* The alliance was concluded after the convention of Hasdrubal and is opposed to the pacific and conciliatory spirit shown at that time by Rome. But Rome had now subdued the Cisalpine Gauls, and was prepared for active intervention in Spain. She interfered in the party conflicts at Saguntum, and thus gave Hannibal a pretext for attacking the town. He met the protests of a Roman embassy with the reply that Saguntum had broken the peace by assaults on the allies of Carthage, and by inviting the intervention of Rome. Perhaps he hoped that Saguntum would yield under pressure, and that Rome, still busy with securing her hold on Illyria and menaced with a flank attack from Macedon, would recede before accomplished facts in the West. In any case he de-

* I have followed Meltzer in disregarding the sophisms of Livy, and in interpreting Polybius in the sense most favourable to the Carthaginians.

termined to finish the work in Spain before he invaded Italy, for he dared not leave Rome a base of operations from which to menace his rear and destroy the Iberian empire of Carthage. But Saguntum displayed that splendid obstinacy in hopeless resistance which in later days marked the defence of Numantia and Sarragossa. For eight months it endured the fierce assaults of Hannibal and Maharbal, and the slow starvation of a rigorous blockade (219 B.C.). Had the Romans shown but a tithe of the energy of their clients, they might easily have relieved Saguntum by invading Spain. But their supine inaction sacrificed their allies, and brought the curse of war to their own gates. At length the ill-fated town was stormed, and perished in the flames kindled by its heroic chieftains.

By this exploit Hannibal bound Spain to him Declaration of War. with the strong cords of love or fear. With the spoils he purchased the adhesion of waverers at Carthage. Roman envoys vainly endeavouring to tamper with the Spanish tribes were treated with the contempt earned by their desertion of Saguntum. Nor did the ambassadors meet with more success at Carthage. Their instructions were simple; they were to demand the surrender of Hannibal and his principal officers for breaking the treaty by the assault on Saguntum, and if this were refused, to declare war. In vain did the Punic senators attempt, by raising the previous question whether Saguntum was an ally of Rome under the terms of the treaty, to justify the action of their general. The time for special pleading on minute questions was now past. The causes of the war were not to be found in the fate, deserved or undeserved, of a Spanish town, but in the high-handed injustice of Rome shown in the seizure of Sardinia, and in the hatred which, beneath an Oriental impassivity, rankled and festered in the heart of Carthage. The struggle for the empire of the Western Mediterranean must be fought out to the bitter end between rival cities, divided by race, by creed, and by the memory of cruel wrongs and misfortunes. Fabius Buteo, the head of the Roman embassy, put in dramatic form the simple question before the Punic Senate. Gathering up his robe in a fold, he exclaimed, ' Behold, here are peace and war: which do you choose?' 'Which you will,' was the answer of the Shofete. And when Fabius shook out the fold and gave them war, the members of the council mustered courage to reply that they welcomed the choice with all their heart.

CHAPTER III

THE RHONE, THE ALPS AND THE TREBIA

THE genius of Hannibal is first clearly seen in Plans of Hannibal. the mingled audacity and prudence of his plan of campaign. Every possible precaution is taken to ensure the safety of Spain and of Africa. He sent 15,000 Spanish troops to hold Africa, and summoned nearly as many Libyans and Numidians to take their place in Spain. Thus each force quartered in a foreign land was cut off from the opportunity of revolt, and served as a hostage for the fidelity of its country. He left his brother Hasdrubal to command in Spain, with 12,500 foot, 2500 horse and 21 elephants, and further handed over to him the whole fleet stationed there, amounting to some 50 quinqueremes. For serious offensive purposes he thought the navy of Carthage inadequate. Two squadrons of 20 or 25 sail were to make a diversion by assaults on the coasts of Italy and Sicily. But the empire of the sea had now passed from the hands of Carthage into those of her rival. Throughout the war we find Roman commanders able to send troops by sea to Spain, to harry the coasts and islands of Africa, to threaten Carthage from the strongholds of Sicily.

Thus actual necessity compelled Hannibal to invade Italy by land. But quite apart from the danger of exposing his army to destruction by a superior enemy on the high seas, many strategic considerations pointed to the valley of the Po as his true base. To strike a blow at the heart of Rome he must first gain a firm foothold in Italy. The Italians and Greeks had now become reconciled to Roman leadership, but the Gallic tribes felt their very existence threatened by the chain of Roman roads and fortresses just fastened upon them. The Boii and Insubres were ready to furnish Hannibal with guides for the march, and with recruits when he should reach Italy. Lastly, Hannibal hoped for the co-operation of Macedon, which through the victory of Sellasia had re-established its suzerainty in Greece, and resented Roman predominance on the Illyrian seaboard. If the armies of Spain and of Macedon were to combine against the legions, their nearest meeting-place was Cisalpine Gaul. It was no spirit of hare-brained adventure, but far-reaching and methodical calculation which led Hannibal over the Alps.

Hannibal's Vision. Hannibal set out from Cartagena in the spring of 218, at the head of 90,000 infantry, 12,000 horse and 37 elephants. He bade farewell for many a year to the Spanish princess he had married and their infant child. His deep sense that he was heaven's instrument for the destruction of his country's foes haunted him by night as well as by day. In his sleep he saw the chief god of his fathers sitting in council with the other deities. From the council he received a solemn charge to invade Italy, and a celestial guide to lead him on his way. Bidden not to look behind him, after a while he could no longer restrain his curiosity. And when he turned, he beheld a monstrous form, thick set all over with serpents, crashing through woods and orchards and houses. And to his question what this might portend, his guide answered, 'Thou seest the desolation of Italy; go forward, and cast no look behind.' So Hannibal, giving up for ever the joys of peace and the comforts of home, went forth to fight to the death with his country's foes.

The difficulties and dangers of the route chosen were soon apparent. Hannibal marched without loss to the Ebro, but the sturdy Catalans beyond opposed the advancing columns stoutly. It cost Hannibal 20,000 men to force his way through their mountainous land; 11,000 more were left under Hanno to hold the country, and about as many more, who were found to be disaffected or discouraged by the prospect of service abroad, were dismissed to their homes. With 50,000 foot and 9000 horse, all veteran soldiers, Hannibal crossed the Pyrenees and pressed swiftly forward to the Rhone. He had smoothed his way by giving fair words and good gold to the Celtic tribes. Speed was of the first importance if he

Hannibal's March from the Ebro to the Rhone.

was to reach the Alps before the passes were closed by snow. But the delay in Catalonia prevented him from arriving on the Rhone near Avignon till the end of August.

Preparations of the Romans. The Romans were as much astonished at the swift audacity of the young general as were the old-fashioned Austrian generals by the brilliant strategy of Frederick or of Napoleon. With half a million of men ready for the call to arms, the Senate was content to enrol but the two ordinary consular armies. One consul, Ti. Sempronius Longus, was assigned 24,400 footmen and 2400 horse, with a fleet of 160 quinqueremes, for a descent on Africa from Sicily; the other, P. Cornelius Scipio, received a force of 22,000 foot, 2200 horse and 60 quinqueremes for service in Spain. A prætor, L. Manlius Volso, was given some 20,000 men to hold down Cisalpine Gaul. Rome had grasped the triple problem of the war, the defence of Cisalpine Gaul, with attacks on Carthage and on the Punic empire in Spain, but like an unskilled boxer she struck feebly and she struck late. A descent in force on Spain and a decisive blow in Africa might have ended the war almost before it had begun. But Sempronius frittered away time and opportunity over minor operations, and Scipio's force was too weak to meet Hannibal in Spain. Further, Scipio's troops were detained in North Italy by a Celtic rising. The Boii and Insubres, excited by Hannibal's emissaries and enraged by the recent foundation of fortress-colonies at Placentia and Cremona, rose in revolt, expelled the Roman colonists, treacherously seized their leaders, and drove the prætor in headlong flight to Tannetum. Scipio was directed to despatch his legions to restore order in North Italy and to raise fresh levies for the Spanish service. Nor did he afterwards strain every nerve to atone for this unfortunate delay. Sailing leisurely along the coast from Pisa, he reached Massilia in August, and there learned to his horror that Hannibal had conquered the Catalans, crossed the Pyrenees, and was marching on the Rhone. Labouring under the fixed idea that the river was impassable, the consul lay inactive at its mouth, and merely despatched 300 horse and a few Gallic irregulars to ascertain the position of the enemy.

Hannibal, when he reached the Rhone near Roquemaure, found no Roman troops ready to dispute his passage. But the influence of the men of Massilia, true as ever to the Roman cause, had induced the neighbouring tribes to band themselves together against the Carthaginian. The Rhone itself was a formidable obstacle for an army without pontoons or boats; to cross it under the eyes of a brave if undisciplined enemy, before Scipio could arrive, might well seem impossible. But Hannibal at once ordered his men to collect boats, and to make rafts and

Hannibal crosses the Rhone.

canoes from felled trees with all speed. In two days he was ready to cross the stream, but he would not risk a front attack on the Gallic host, preferring to turn their position by a flank march and a surprise. During the night he sent off a detachment under his trusted lieutenant Hanno, with orders to ascend the right bank for about five-and-twenty miles, and thus secure a passage where there was no enemy to stop them. Taking advantage of one of the many islands in that part of the Rhone, Hanno's force crossed the divided stream on barks and rafts, and after a day's rest, moved down to take the Gauls in rear.

Meanwhile Hannibal had completed his preparations. The heaviest vessels were placed highest up stream, to break the force of the mighty river, swollen with the melting snows of the Alps. These larger craft held the cavalry, whose horses were towed behind, while the flower of the infantry was on board the boats. At length Hannibal saw a column of smoke rising on the further shore, the preconcerted signal which told him of Hanno's arrival, and instantly ordered his men to embark and pull rapidly across the stream. Behind them rose the cheers of their friends and comrades; in front the Gauls greeted them with war songs and shouts of defiance. The barbarians expected an easy victory, but suddenly found their camp in flames behind them, and Hanno's horsemen charging them in flank and rear. Surprised and bewildered, they made but a feeble resistance to the landing of Hannibal, and fled in confusion as soon as he attacked them with the first troops he could form on the bank. Before night fell Hannibal had conveyed his whole force except his elephants across the Rhone. The passage of the elephants was a longer and more difficult matter. Large rafts covered with earth were fastened· to the bank; to these were attached smaller rafts, also covered with earth, which in turn were joined by towing lines to a number of the largest barks. When the elephants had been enticed on to the smaller rafts by two female decoys, these were at once cut loose and towed across the river. Though some of the frightened beasts plunged overboard and drowned their drivers, they are said all to have reached the bank uninjured.

While Hannibal lay yet on the Rhone, waiting The First for the elephants to cross, two significant events Encounter occurred. The chieftains of the Insubres and Romans. other Cisalpine Gauls reached his camp eager to encourage him on his way. Speaking to the assembled army through interpreters, they undertook to show them the shortest and safest route across the Alps, and painted in glowing colours the riches of the valley of the Po and the zeal of its inhabitants for the Punic cause. Finally Hannibal himself urged on the soldiers the need

of undaunted courage and implicit confidence in
their leader.   Scarcely had the assembly dispersed,
when the 500 Numidians, sent down the Rhone
to reconnoitre by Hannibal, were seen riding
hard towards the camp in full flight before
the enemy.   They had encountered the Roman
and Gallic horse detached by Scipio, and after
a sharp skirmish had beaten a hasty retreat.
Whether the Numidian light horse were really
unable to meet the shock of the heavier Roman
troopers, or whether they acted under orders in
drawing on the enemy to the verge of the camp,
and leading them to believe Hannibal's forces were
still divided by the Rhone, cannot now be determined.   In any case the report of the Roman
officer caused Scipio to march his whole army up
the Rhone in the hope of encountering Hannibal.
He found only a deserted camp, and returned to
Marseilles, reviling the cowardice of an enemy,
who had made use of his three days' start to
elude his pursuer.   The consul had wasted a week,
and wearied his troops to no purpose; he still
had the advantage of free communication by sea
both with Spain and Italy.   A bolder leader
might have at once embarked for Genoa, to
muster every available man in North Italy and
fling his whole force at Hannibal as he emerged
exhausted from the passes of the Alps.   Scipio
did not so read the situation.   Acting probably
on orders from the Senate, he sent his army to

Spain under the command of his brother and lieutenant, Cn. Scipio, and himself set sail for Pisa, intending to take command of the force of Manlius, and to make head against Hannibal in Cisalpine Gaul. The wisdom of this resolution has been vigorously canvassed. Undoubtedly the iron tenacity with which the Scipios and their successors maintained the struggle in Spain prevented the consolidation of the Punic power there, and the despatch thence of reinforcements which might have enabled Hannibal to end the struggle in Italy. But might not Hannibal himself have been crushed, if Scipio had concentrated his whole force in Cisalpine Gaul?

Hannibal had never intended to give battle to the Roman legions on the Rhone. To free himself from the danger of an attack in flank, he marched four days up the river to the island of the Allobroges, that is, the rich plain at the confluence of the Rhone and the Isère. Here he found two brothers contending for the chieftainship of the tribe. Hannibal won the gratitude of the elder brother by deciding the dispute in his favour, and received in return for his good offices a plentiful supply of food, clothing and other necessaries for his men. The course of his march from this point over the Alps has been the subject of much ingenious if inconclusive controversy. The solution of the question must be sought rather from Alpine and military experts than from

The Passes of the Alps.

historians. Hannibal's object was to find the
shortest and easiest route by which a regular army,
accompanied by a baggage-train and elephants,
could make its way from the valley of the Rhone
to that of the Po. His difficulties were enhanced
by the inevitable vagueness and inaccuracy of his
information, by the lateness of the season (October),
and by the necessity of evading Scipio's army,
which threw him off the direct route up the valley
of the Durance (Druentia). Doubtless he had
undervalued the risks of a project planned with
the deliberate audacity of genius. On the other
hand, we must neither exaggerate the difficulties
nor read into the accounts our own topographical
knowledge. The choice for Hannibal lay between
two great valleys, each of which leads to two
practicable passes. The southern roads, either by
the Cornice or the Col di Tenda, may be at once
rejected as bringing Hannibal far too near the
coast; similarly the north-eastern passes (Great
St Bernard or Simplon) would imply an incredibly
difficult and circuitous route. The real question
is between (1) the Isère, leading to the Little St
Bernard (7076 ft.); (2) its tributary, the Arc, leading to Mont Cenis (6859 ft.); (3) the Durance, ascending to Mont Genèvre (6101 ft.); (4) its feeder,
the Ubaye, which leads to the Col d'Argentière
(6538 ft.). All of these passes seem to have been
used in antiquity either by regular armies or by
migratory tribes; all are sufficiently easy to be

possible, but hard enough before the existence of
roads or bridges to account for the sufferings and
dangers of the march.

There can be little doubt that Hannibal had Which
originally intended to make his way to Italy by Pass did
the valley of the Durance. But the dangerous choose?
proximity of the Roman army compelled him
to move up the Rhone to its junction with the
Isère. So far our authorities Polybius and Livy
are agreed. But from this point their differences
can hardly be reconciled. Livy clearly believed
that Hannibal turned aside to the country of the
Tricorii and Tricastini, that is, that he marched
by Grenoble and the river Drac to the upper valley
of the Durance. Polybius, whose authority on
purely historical questions is paramount, is most
unfortunately vague and inaccurate on points of
geography. His self-complacent assertions of
superior knowledge cannot hide the facts that his
conception of the lie of the mountains and the
course of the Rhone is fundamentally erroneous,
that his descriptions are dull colourless and irre-
concilable with modern maps, and that the
absence of tribal names from his pages makes it
impossible to check his plausible generalities.
The ordinary interpretation of Polybius takes
Hannibal from the Isère eighty miles up the
Rhone to Vienne, thence across the Mont de
Chat by the Lac du Bourget and Chambery, back
to the stream of the Isère and so up the valley

over the Little St Bernard. In favour of this
route are urged the statement of Polybius that
Hannibal began to climb the Alps near the
Rhone after ascending the river, and the times
and distances given by that historian. Against it
there is the obvious improbability that Hannibal
should march round two sides of a triangle to
reach a higher longer and steeper pass. Again,
its summit does not command a view of a sunny
plain, but looks straight on the icy mass of Mont
Blanc; the descending path does not lead straight
down to the plains in which the Taurini and
Insubres dwelt, but debouches by a long and
dangerous defile upon the wild country of the
Salassi. Finally, that Hannibal having reached the
Insubrian country, and knowing that Scipio lay
in the front of him near Placentia, should turn
back to assail Turin is most improbable. The conclusion would seem to follow that we must in this
case prefer the clear consistent and picturesque
narrative of Livy to the indistinct and indefinite
account of Polybius. In fine, Hannibal crossed the
Alps either by the Durance and Mont Genèvre,
or by the Ubaye and the Col d'Argentière. Most
probably he chose the former, for the ascent by
the valley of the Durance is the easier, the pass
lower, and the descending path would lead him
directly upon the land of the Taurini.

The
Ascent of
the Alps.
From Grenoble, Hannibal made his way without
serious difficulty up the valley of the Drac. But

when he attempted to pass into that of the
Panerasse, and so reach the line of the Durance,
he found the defile occupied by the mountaineers.
He learned, however, from his Gaulish guides that
the tribesmen, when night came on, were in the
habit of retiring to the fortified village in the
valley behind them. Hannibal, having lulled the
barbarians into a false security by ostentatiously
encamping in their sight, afterwards, when they
withdrew at nightfall, seized the abandoned defile.
When day dawned, the outwitted mountaineers
found their positions occupied, and the Punic army
marching past, but as they noted the long line of
horses and baggage animals struggling along the
mountain side, they could not refrain from a fierce
assault, prompted by desire of plunder. Rushing
down the mountain, they threw the Carthaginian
column into confusion, heightened by the plunging
of wounded horses and terrified baggage cattle.
Nor could order be restored till Hannibal's picked
troops, who held the crest of the heights, charged
down and drove off the barbarians with a storm
of missiles. After taking the town, Hannibal
marched forward by Chorges to Embrun, on the
Upper Durance. Beyond that place the natives
met him unarmed, with branches in their hands,
and offered supplies guides and hostages. Hannibal, though mistrustful of their good faith, was
compelled to accept their guidance along a path
which now climbed almost inaccessible hills, and

now wound through a gorge on a narrow ledge beneath precipitous rocks and above a furious torrent. Dreading the dangers of these defiles, he sent forward his elephants and cavalry with the baggage, and himself covered the march with his infantry. When his troops were thoroughly entangled in the gorge, suddenly boulders and stones were hurled down on their devoted heads from the cliffs above, and a stream of barbarians poured down on the convoy in the centre of the column, and cut the Punic army in half. But meanwhile Hannibal had seized, with his infantry, a white rock commanding the defile, and by well directed yolleys of darts, forced the barbarians to relinquish their prey. Without further difficulty he made his way by Briançon to the summit of the pass, and from the heights of Mont Genèvre, showed his troops the easy descent that led to the plains of Italy. 'You stand,' he said, 'triumphant on its ramparts; one or two easy victories will secure you full possession.' Yet even after a rest of two days, the weary and dispirited soldiers were with difficulty animated to fresh exertions by the burning enthusiasm of their general.

The Descent from the Summit. The descent began on the 29th of October. Though no further obstacles were thrown in the way by the Alpine clans, the natural difficulties of the steep descent rivalled those of the ascent. At last the vanguard was confronted by a yawning chasm, where an avalanche or landslip had carried

away the track for three hundred yards. To
advance was impossible, to go round over the
treacherous masses of fresh snow, where men and
animals slipped down the steep mountain side, or
were engulfed in the drifts, proved equally im-
practicable. Hannibal was obliged to encamp for
the night on that slippery crest. Next day he
set his men to work by relays hewing a path
along the wall of the chasm. Every man was
working for dear life, and in a single day the road
was so far restored that horses and pack animals
could go down it to pastures below the snow-line.
Three days more made it wide and solid enough
for the half-famished elephants. Hannibal, who
had stayed with the rear-guard, overtook his
cavalry and baggage, and in three days reached,
unopposed, the plain of Piedmont. But he had
sacrificed the larger half of his army to gain his
chosen field of battle. He had crossed the
Pyrenees at the head of an army of 50,000 infantry
and 9000 horse; there remained after crossing the
Alps but 20,000 footmen and 6000 horse. Nor
was this all. The horses were worn out, the
elephants starving, the men exhausted with toil
and squalid with neglect. Yet with this handful
of heroic 'shadows' Hannibal was to attack and
conquer the fresh troops and innumerable reserves of Roman Italy.

Hannibal had reached Italy by an unexpected Scipio's
route with surprising speed, while the Roman Strategy.

armies that should have met him were in Spain and Sicily. Sempronius, though doubtless already recalled by the Senate, could not hope to reach the field of war at once. Scipio had sent his own legions to Spain, and had under his command only the troops of Manlius and Atilius, which were barely strong enough to keep down the Gauls. Doubtful of professed friends and certain of many enemies, he did not attempt to close the passes of the Alps. He could not know by which line Hannibal would come; thus to concentrate his troops would have been to lay himself open to a turning movement and an insurrection in his rear; to scatter them was to court certain defeat by a stronger force. But if he was not ready to hold the passes of the Alps, he should have stood on the defensive behind the Po. He had landed at Pisa, crossed the Apennines, and in two months, at the head of the legions of Italy, had restored order on the right bank of the river. Had he made Placentia his base, and occupied the famous Stradella pass, he would have compelled Hannibal to give battle under the most unfavourable conditions. But the consul remembered too well the superiority of Roman soldiers in the first Punic war, and the successful skirmish on the Rhone, to feel any anxiety in pushing on with raw troops to encounter Hannibal's weary veterans. Hannibal also was eager for the fray. He had rested his army for some time among the friendly Insubres, and by a vigorous assault had stormed Taurasia, and thus terrified the Taurini and other hostile tribes into submission. He now heard with grim delight that Scipio had crossed the Po, and was moving forward over a plain on which his weak cavalry was at the mercy of the Punic horse. By a striking object lesson he strove to teach his troops that their choice lay between victory and death. He asked his Celtic prisoners if they would fight with one another to the death on condition that the victors should receive freedom and honours. The brave barbarians with one voice professed their readiness to accept the offer, and congratulated those of their comrades who were selected as combatants in these deadly duels. Hannibal's veterans were not less ready to snatch freedom and victory from the very jaws of death.

Both generals were anxious by rapid success to ensure the adherence of the wavering and divided Gallic clans. Each pushed forward with his vanguard to reconnoitre the numbers and position of the enemy. Hannibal crossed the Sesia with 6000 horsemen, and suddenly met the consul at the head of about 3000 horse and a corps of light infantry on the nearer bank of the Ticinus. The combat that followed, called with some exaggeration the battle of the Ticinus, was short sharp and decisive. Hannibal posted his heavy cavalry in the centre and his Numidians on the wings, the consul drew up his light infantry in front and his horsemen in

The Battle on the Ticinus.

support. But the raw infantry gave way before the first charge of Hannibal's Spanish horsemen, and though Scipio's Gallic cavalry stood their ground, they were outflanked and taken in the rear by the Numidians, whose movements decided the conflict. The consul himself was severely wounded, and owed his life to the courage of his son, who lived to end at Zama the war so unfortunately begun on the Ticinus.

Scipio and Hannibal.
Scipio saw at once that with inferior cavalry his position on the plain of Lombardy was untenable. He beat a hasty retreat, broke down the bridge he had made over the Po, and with the sacrifice of 600 men left behind to cover his retreat across the river, fell back on his true line of defence under the walls of Placentia. Here the Roman fortresses Placentia and Cremona commanded the passage of the Po, supported and supplied the àrmy in the field, and enabled the consul to curb the discontented Gauls, and await in safety the arrival of his colleague. When Hannibal found that Scipio had escaped him, he did not march down the north bank of the Po, since an advance on this line would have led him into the country of the Cenomani, friends and allies of Rome, and would have obliged him to cross the great river in face of the enemy. He therefore ascended the Po on the northern bank, crossed the river by a bridge of boats, and then, with his numbers swelled by Celtic insurgents, pushed down the stream to seize the Stradella

pass and confront the Roman army near Placentia. He was most anxious to provoke a general action, and crush one consular army before the other could reach the field; only a victory would secure him the unanimous support of the Gauls, with supplies and quarters for the winter. Scipio prudently refused battle, and patiently awaited the coming of his colleague.

For Sempronius was now marching with extraordinary rapidity to North Italy. He had spent the summer in unprofitable descents on the islands round Sicily, which could have no decisive effect on the fortunes of the war. Ordered to invade Africa, he had suffered his great fleet and army to be paralysed by the small Punic squadrons despatched to threaten Italy and Sicily. Accident had revealed the Carthaginian plans to Hiero, king of Syracuse; and through his timely warning the prætor, M. Æmilius, was enabled to baffle an attempt to surprise the town of Lilybæum, and by sheer hard fighting to repulse the Punic fleet off the port. But even when Sempronius arrived with 160 ships, the Carthaginian squadrons kept the sea, and detained him in the neighbourhood of Sicily. The capture of Malta was the only success he could boast when he was hastily recalled by the Senate to meet Hannibal. Leaving the bulk of his fleet to protect the coasts of Sicily and South Italy, the consul sailed for Rome. His soldiers, bound by a solemn oath to meet

Sempron-
ius in
Sicily.

D

their leader at Ariminum, accomplished their long march thither in forty days.

The Carthaginian and Roman armies were thus all converging on the plain of the Po, at the point where that river is joined by the Trebia. The position of this stream and of Placentia is the key to the subsequent operations. The Trebia in winter pours down from its mountain gorge a furious torrent, but in the plain it spreads over a broad and pebbly bed. Through this plain, which is in places furrowed by ravines, the river flows for seven miles until it joins the Po, some two miles above Placentia. Like many Italian streams, it is nearly dry in summer, and even in winter generally fordable, but after heavy rain in the mountains it flows with a strong and turbulent flood.

The real difficulty is to determine on which side of the Trebia the armies lay. We are told by Polybius that Hannibal encamped five miles from Scipio, and while in this position received envoys from the Boii, who dwelt near Parma, between Placentia and Ariminium. Then Scipio, alarmed by a mutiny among his Gallic auxiliaries, and thinking his lines on the plain threatened by Hannibal's superior cavalry, retreated by night across the Trebia to a stronger position on a spur of the Apennines. The Numidians were ordered by Hannibal, who started in hot pursuit, to harass and delay the march of the enemy, but they wasted time in burning the deserted Roman camp, and allowed Scipio to escape to his new entrenchment. Here the two armies again confronted each other, divided by the stream of the Trebia. While they occupied these positions, Sempronius, marching from Ariminum, effected a junction with his colleague without opposition, and Hannibal captured the Roman fortress and granary at Clastidium, twenty miles to the west of the Trebia. Considerations of strategy would seem to prove that Scipio's first camp was on the left bank of the Trebia, connected with Placentia by a bridge of boats, and that he retired eastward to the hills across the stream, thus protecting his front, and covering his communications with Ariminum and his junction with Sempronius. Indeed, it is difficult to see how Hannibal could have allowed Sempronius to reach his colleague's camp unopposed, or could have drawn his supplies from Clastidium after its capture, had he once seized a position between the two consuls. On the other hand, the weight of ancient authority (for the vaguer testimony of Polybius, though leaving the crucial question unanswered, seems to confirm rather than contradict the clear statement of Livy) and the silent witness of topography point to the conclusion that Scipio first encamped behind the Trebia close to the walls of Placentia, and afterwards crossed to seek the shelter of the hills on its left bank, while Hannibal threw himself across his communications with Rome and Ariminum. Both theories are open to grave objections, though the balance of probability would seem to be in favour of the former.

Sempron-
ius.
In any case there is not much doubt as to the general course of the campaign or the tactics of the battle. Sempronius eluded Hannibal and reached his colleague's camp by forced marches early in December. Anxious to crown his fast expiring consulship with a notable exploit, confident in superior numbers and in the valour of his legionaries, he was as eager as Hannibal to fight a pitched battle. Scipio's masterly inactivity in an unassailable position was the true policy for Rome, the policy that in later years baffled and ruined Hannibal. At this juncture it would have forced him to try the fickle Gauls by imposing on them the burden of supporting his army in winter quarters, or to venture on a dangerous flank march past the Roman camp. But Sempronius saw only that the few Gauls yet faithful to Rome were being alienated by the ravages of Hannibal's cavalry. He crossed the Trebia, drove in the plundering Numidians, and, puffed up with an easy victory, conceded by the orders of Hannibal, determined to follow up his success by a general action.

The Battle
of the
Trebia.
The wily Carthaginian rejoiced to see his enemy ready to sacrifice the advantages of a strong defensive position, and to fall into the snare cunningly devised to tempt the impetuous ardour of the rash and inexperienced consul. In the

hollow of a ravine behind his chosen field of battle he placed an ambush of 2000 picked men, horse

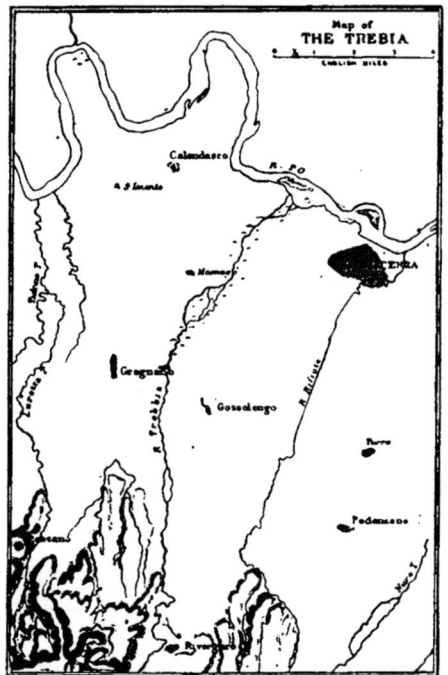

and foot, hidden by the brushwood and the banks under the command of his younger brother, Mago. Next morning, on a cold December day, while snow and rain were falling driven by a wintry wind, and the Trebia was rolling in full flood down its pebbly channel, the Numidians, by skirmishing with the enemy's light infantry, drew the whole Roman army, horse and foot, across the stream. The soldiers were famished, since they had not

been given time for their morning meal, and numb
with cold, for the icy stream through which they
waded was running breast-high. Hannibal, anxious
to make his victory complete, suffered the whole
host to pass the stream and reach the plain. But
the hungry and shivering legionaries had to face
a well-fed and well-warmed army. Further, they
had to fight with a river in their rear, on an open
plain, outflanked by the superior Carthaginian
cavalry. Hannibal's heavy footmen were formed
in phalanx in the centre, covered by his skirmishers and slingers in front, and by his cavalry
and elephants on both flanks. The legions took
their usual order, with the cavalry on the wings.
At the first encounter the Roman light troops
were routed by the Phœnician skirmishers and
Baliaric slingers. With equal ease their weak
cavalry was dispersed by Hannibal's horse and
elephants. Nevertheless, the heavy infantry proved
itself worthy of its reputation, for the legionaries
closed boldly with the enemy, and in spite of all,
maintained at least an equal fight. But the slingers
smote them with a storm of missiles, the cavalry
and elephants, falling upon both flanks, trampled
them down, and to crown their misfortunes, Mago
with his chosen band broke out from his ambush
and assailed them furiously in rear. Yet the
legions in the centre, 10,000 strong, cut their way
right through the Punic line, and marched off in
good order to Placentia. Of the rest, many dis-

persed, many were slaughtered at the passage of the river, where the pursuit was stayed owing to the piercing cold. Only the wreck of an army reached the Roman camp, and was led by Scipio under cover of night to the safe refuge of Placentia.

The victory of the Trebia is a masterpiece of skill in itself enough to stamp Hannibal as a great tactician. With but trifling loss, chiefly in Celtic auxiliaries, Hannibal had destroyed 20,000 Romans, and annihilated their army as an organised effective force. He was master of Cisalpine Gaul, and enlisted 60,000 Celtic clansmen under his banner. But the cruel cold of a Lombard winter decimated his veterans, worn already with disease and privations, and killed all but one of his elephants. The inclemency of the season forbade any serious attack on the Roman fortresses, and forced him to give up the attempt to cross the Apennines. He was therefore obliged to winter in Cisalpine Gaul, and spent his time partly in assaults on the Roman outposts, but mainly in organising his new levies. Yet he dare not trust to the fidelity of a race notoriously fickle and treacherous. By the constant use of disguises he gained much valuable information as to the temper of his new followers, and eluded the danger of assassination. Much had been accomplished in a single campaign. By a sudden attack Hannibal had disconcerted the offensive

Results of the First Campaign.

projects of Rome, and compelled superior forces to stand on the defensive. He had outwitted at every turn the stout soldiers opposed to him, and had crowned his work by the utter defeat of the united Roman armies on a fair field. Sempronius, hurrying back to Rome for the elections, escaped as by a miracle the squadrons of the enemy. Scipio was glad to convey the relics of his force down the Po, and so by sea to Ariminum. Hannibal was now firmly established in the valley of the Po, but if he was ever to master the might of Rome, he must bring the war to her very gates, and undermine the true foundations of her power by sapping the loyalty of her Italian allies.

CHAPTER IV

THE BATTLES OF LAKE TRASIMENE AND CANNÆ

AT Rome, as the real truth concerning the battle on the Trebia became known, alarm rose to actual fear for the safety of the city. In vain had the official bulletins stated that the consul had been robbed of his victory by the severity of a winter storm. The people realised that the recent defeat was more disastrous than any that had befallen them since the disgraceful calamity of the Caudine Forks. They were the more determined to elect to the consulship the ensuing year a man after their own heart, the vehement leader of the popular party, C. Flaminius. As tribune (232 B.C.) he had won the gratitude of the populace by carrying a law for the division of the land once held by the Senonian Gauls among poor citizens. As censor (220 B.C.) he had given employment to many on the great Flaminian road to Ariminum and on his circus in Rome. But his law had encountered the interested opposition of the senatorial capitalists who occupied public land, and his support of a tribun-

--

ician proposal, which excluded senators from the shipping trade (218 B.C.), added fuel to the fires of aristocratic hatred. In his earlier consulship (223 B.C.), while engaged in a war with the Insubres, he had received a sealed letter from the Senate recalling him on the pretence that a defect in the auspices had vitiated his election. Flaminius left the letter unopened till he had won the impending battle, and then replied that the gods had ratified his election by giving him the victory. Though his success was due, not to the blundering strategy of the general, which compelled him to accept battle with a river in his rear, but to the staunchness of his troops, the people, in spite of the Senate's refusal, insisted on voting him a triumph. The Senate afterwards took its revenge for the rebuff by obliging him to resign the mastership of the horse, because a mouse had been heard to squeak at his nomination.

And now again the heavens lightened and thundered, showered hailstones and rained blood, for terror gave birth to portents, and was in turn increased by them. But Flaminius scoffed at the superstitious fears of the multitude and the chicanery of aristocratic priests, who hoped by means of these dread omens to prevent his entry upon the consulship to which he had been elected. Disregarding the customary ceremonies, he left Rome abruptly, and in spite of a message of recall from the Senate, assumed the command of the army at Ariminum. Pursued by threatening portents, he led his legions to Arretium, while his colleague, Cn. Servilius, took post at Ariminum, and Scipio proceeded to Spain.

The Roman preparations for the coming Roman campaign were vigorous and adequate. Troops Position. were despatched to Sicily, Sardinia, and Spain, the garrisons on the Italian coast were increased, and 60 quinqueremes added to the fleet. Four new legions were levied, which, with the remnants of the army beaten at the Trebia, occupied Ariminum and Arretium. Servilius with his main force at Ariminum blocked the Flaminian road, and by outposts at Cremona and Placentia, threatened Cisalpine Gaul. Flaminius at Arretium commanded the Upper Arno and the passes of the Apennines, while detachments at Lucca and Pisa watched the coast road and the lower course of the river. The position of the Roman armies was much the same as when, eight years before, they awaited a Gallic invasion ; it was turned, as then, by a bold and unexpected flanking movement.

Hannibal had long determined to transfer the war Hannibal from the valley of the Po to Central Italy. The transfers Gauls were already weary of maintaining his army, the War. but might still be trusted to join in any campaign which promised plunder. The Carthaginian felt that his country compared unfavourably both in the will and the power to fight with the iron constancy and the inexhaustible resources of Rome. To triumph over such a city, it was necessary to

discredit Roman rule by the utter discomfiture of
the generals and the legions opposed to him, and
to win the hearts of the Italian subjects as their
champion against the oppression of the dominant
state. For both purposes a base in Italy itself
was essential, since Gaul was too distant and too
foreign to serve his purpose. Accordingly Hannibal prepared the way for his second campaign by
a stroke of policy aimed at the Roman alliance.
While he loaded the Roman citizens among his
prisoners with chains, he sent the Italians to their
homes to announce the coming of one who would
deliver them from their bondage to Rome.

Hannibal crosses the Marshes. In the spring he crossed the Apennines, not, as
it would appear, by the ordinary road along the
Macra, nor yet from Bononia to Pistoria, but by
the more difficult route along the Auser or Serchio.
Debouching from the hills somewhere between
Lucca and Pescia, he pushed straight across the
floods and marshes that cover the lower valleys of
the Arno and Serchio. For four days and three
nights the army toiled through the vast swamp, unable to find a dry spot for rest or sleep. Hannibal
ordered his Libyan and Spanish veterans to lead
the way, and Mago, with the cavalry, to bring up
the rear. In the centre the unfortunate Gauls
stumbled over the trampled morass, driven back to
their post by Mago's horsemen if they tried to desert.
The sufferings and losses both in men and horses
of the army were severe ; the leader himself had one

of his eyes blinded by ophthalmia. But he completely eluded the observation of the Roman outposts, and emerged triumphant on the flank of the opposing armies somewhere between Empoli and Florence. Servilius was still far away at Ariminum, and Flaminius lay quietly at Arretium.

Hannibal now marched rapidly past the left flank of the Roman army, probably by way of Siena, towards Cortona, and completely turned the position of Flaminius. By this masterly manœuvre he baffled the Senate's plan of defence, and interposed between the Roman army and the capital. Anxious to provoke his headstrong opponent to battle, he laid waste the rich valley of the Clanis with fire and sword. Flaminius was obliged to dog his opponent's footsteps if he would save Italy from devastation and the unprotected city from panic. Further, every rule of strategy demanded that he should seek to join his colleague as he retreated by the Flaminian way, at some point in the neighbourhood of Perugia. If the two consuls could crush Hannibal between their converging armies, or fall with their united force on his rear, they might yet make him repent the apparent rashness with which he had sacrificed his line of communication. But Flaminius was not the man to conduct this delicate and difficult operation. He did not indeed, as partisan annalists affirm, from selfish ambition and mortified pride force on a battle in his colleague's absence, but he fell blindly into the

Hannibal advances pursued by Flaminius.

snare skilfully prepared for him by the craftiest
of all great captains. He saw only the hated
Africans rioting in the plundered garden of Italy,
and pressed forward to avenge the insult; he never
dreamed that the enemy he so hotly pursued was
already crouching in ambush ready for the deadly
spring which should destroy another Roman army.
He was not so small a man as to risk his country's
destruction through a jealous desire to keep all the
honour of success for himself, or through a baseless
confidence in his own genius, but as a general he
was rash and incompetent enough to neglect the ele-
mentary duties of concerting a plan of action with
his colleague and of scouting along his line of march.

Lake
Trasimene.
Flaminius pushed hastily forward from Arretium
past Cortona, and encamped late in the evening
by the side of Lake Trasimene. That broad but
shallow mere is girdled with considerable hills.
The road from Cortona to Perugia runs along its
northern shore over low-lying marshy ground.
But at two points the hills come down almost to
the margin of the lake, leaving but a narrow passage for the road. The first projecting ridge is
known as Monte Gualandro, the second forms the
long and narrow defile by Passignano. Between
these points the hills recede in a semi-circle, leaving what seems a spreading plain by contrast with
the narrow entrance and outlet. But this little
plain itself is broken into two halves by the high
ground near Tuoro. There can be no real doubt

that Livy placed the battle he so vividly describes on the northern margin of the lake; whether Polybius should be reconciled with the Latin historian by a somewhat forced interpretation of his words, or intends to assert that the site of the battle was on the eastern shore, where the road turns up from the lake towards Magione, may be disputable, but it seems certain that the fatal trap into which the Roman army fell was before Passignano.*

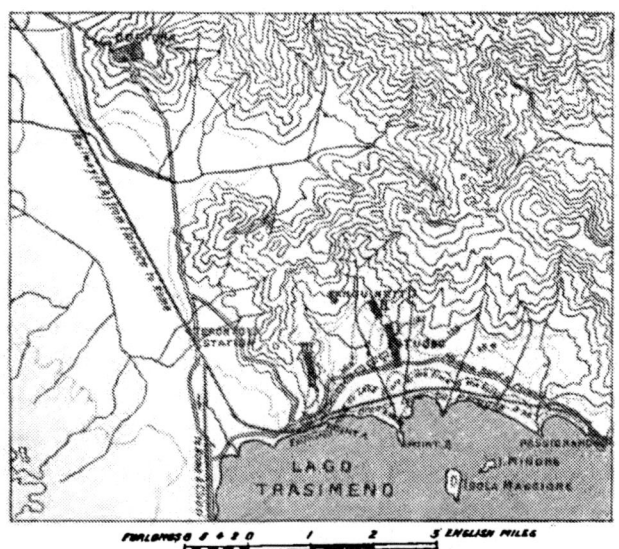

POSITIONS OF CARTHAGINIAN TROOPS.
I. Iberians and Libyans. II. Balearians and Spearmen. III. Cavalry and Celts.

* For a full discussion of the site of the battle, see Mr Grundy, whom I follow, and Mr Henderson in the *Journal of Philology*, 1896-8. Mr Henderson's site looked to my eye far too small considering the numbers and the formation of the troops engaged.

The Battle of Lake Trasimene. Apparently Hannibal himself took his post with the heavy infantry on the hill of Tuoro, while he concealed his Baliaric slingers and light troops behind the higher ridges north of Tuoro, and placed his cavalry and the Gauls in ambush under Monte Gualandro, ready to fall on the Roman rear. In the early hours of an April morning, Flaminius, without waiting even to send forward an advance guard, led his troops into the defile. A thick mist shrouded the lake and the lowlands, but the crests of the hills were clear. Hannibal's troops listened with eager expectation to the tramp of the Roman legions marching blindly into the snare set for them. When the rear of the column was rounding the point of Gualandro, Hannibal gave the signal for a general attack. In a moment the stillness of the morning mist was broken by war cries on every side. The Gauls and the cavalry blocked the entrance to the pass, the heavy infantry, which barred the advance of the Roman column, with the aid of the light troops also assailed its flanks, and drove the disordered masses into the lake. The Roman vanguard alone escaped from the shambles by cutting their way through the troops in front, and reached the hills beyond. The main army had no room to form in line of battle, and barely time to brace up their armour and draw their swords. Yet for three hours they fought on stubbornly, unable to hear an order or see a signal. Flaminius himself strove hard to retrieve the fortune of the day. Run through the body by a Gallic lance, he atoned as far as in him lay for his errors as a general by dying a soldier's death. Such was the fury of the combatants that an earthquake rolled by unheeded. But it was rather a massacre than a battle. Thousands of Romans were cut down where they stood; many, weighed down by their armour, sank in the waters of the lake; thousands were speared or captured by the pursuing cavalry. Even the brave vanguard, which had cut its way to a neighbouring village, was next day caught and compelled to surrender by Maharbal. At the cost of but 1500 men Hannibal had utterly annihilated one of the Roman armies. He crowned his victory by a further success which crippled the other consul. Maharbal, active as ever with the cavalry and light troops, cut to pieces a force of 4000 horsemen sent forward by Servilius to assist his colleague. Hannibal had taken in all some 15,000 prisoners. Summoning them before him, he told those who had surrendered to Maharbal that his lieutenant had no authority to grant them more than their bare lives. He then, with something of Napoleon's vehemence, inveighed against the oppressive government of Rome, and promised the Italians his aid in casting off the yoke. Finally, as at the Trebia, he set the Italians free without ransom, but kept the Romans in custody. Yet if he was stern to the living he did not war with the dead, but vainly sought for the body of the fallen consul that he might give him honourable burial.

At Rome, no attempt was made to hide the gravity of the disaster. The prætor, M. Pomponius Matho, simply announced to the assembled multitude, 'We have been beaten in a great battle.' The few survivors who reached the city, by telling of the death of the consul and the destruction of the army, added to the general terror. But the Senate never wavered nor lost its presence of mind. Day after day it sat from sunrise to sunset in earnest consultation. Even when the loss of Servilius's cavalry became known, it would not withdraw a single man from Spain or Sicily, and simply determined to remedy the evils of the divided command by reviving the dictatorship. In the absence of the surviving consul, Q. Fabius Maximus was elected dictator, and M. Minucius master of the horse, by the Assembly of the Centuries. Fabius was a man destitute indeed of genius, but plentifully endowed with sagacity and common sense. A patrician of the bluest blood, he reverenced authority and tradition, and despised popular opinion. Too proud to listen to the advice òr bow to the will of others, he exhibited a firmness which at times degenerated into obstinacy, and a caution which often bordered on timidity. But he was just the man to save Rome in her hour of need, and to check the flowing tide of Hannibal's success. By

avoiding pitched battles, yet constantly weakening
and harassing the enemy with skirmishes, Fabius
hoped to wear out the invading army, and triumph
by patient endurance. His first measures were
characteristic and effective. To restore confidence
in the city, the angry gods were propitiated by
vows and offerings, and the walls and towers of
Rome repaired and manned. To hinder Hannibal's advance, bridges were broken down, and
the country laid waste wherever he was expected.
Finally, the army in the field was recalled, and
reinforced with two new legions, while men of the
lower orders and freedmen were enrolled to man
the walls of the city, and serve as marines on
board the fleet. Servilius, after handing over his
legions to the dictator, was sent to sea with every
vessel he could muster at Ostia, to meet the
Carthaginian squadron now cruising off Etruria.

Hannibal meanwhile had marched past Perusia
on Spoletium. But that Latin colony had the
courage to close its gates and beat off the attack
of the Punic troops. Taught by this reverse, and
mindful of the weary siege of Saguntum, Hannibal
refrained from uselessly flinging his troops against
the strong walls of Rome. He was entirely without a siege train, he was in a country where
every man was a soldier and an enemy, he had
to face a people whose strength and spirit was
still unbroken. To risk all in a desperate assault
on the capital would have been madness. It is

The March and Plan of Hannibal.

more difficult to say why Hannibal did not fall upon Servilius as he retired along the Flaminian way towards Spoletium. He may have feared to expose an army in which men and horses alike were wasted with disease to a double attack from Rome, now but a few marches distant, and the retreating consul. More probably he foresaw that if attacked, Servilius would fall back on Ariminum, and thus draw him away from his true objective in South Italy to his abandoned base in the valley of the Po. Gaul had proved but a broken reed, and even after Trasimene, Etruria gave no sign. Hannibal's hopes now centred on the warlike Sabellian tribes, and principally on those old enemies of Rome, the Samnites. He wished also to re-establish his connections with Carthage, and open the way for Macedonian aid by taking up a commanding position on the Adriatic. Accord-. ingly, by an unexpected movement he crossed over the Apennines into Picenum, marking his path to the sea with fire and sword. The statement of Polybius, that he expressly ordered the death of every Roman or Latin capable of bearing arms, is discredited by the silence of Livy and the inherent improbability that Hannibal, who spared the lives of soldiers taken in battle, should slaughter an unarmed and inoffensive population. When after ten days he reached the coast, he sent his first official despatch by sea to Carthage, and by the news of his brilliant victories roused the enthusiasm of all parties in the State. In the plains of Picenum, the weary troops and horses lived on the fat of the land, and regained the health and strength lost in their toilsome and unhealthy marches over the snows of the Alps and the swamps of the Arno. Here, too, Hannibal re-armed his African infantry in Roman fashion with the spoils of his late victory. That Hannibal should have ventured the experiment in a hostile country is indeed a striking proof of the superiority of the Roman equipment. When he had thus recruited and reorganised his army, he moved leisurely along the coast, ravaging the land as he went, and at length encamped near Arpi, in Apulia. But not a single city accepted his proffered alliance, or opened its gates to the invader. The blessings of local self-government, the nascent sentiment of Italian nationality, the fear still inspired by the name of Rome, kept her allies true to their allegiance. And within a short time Fabius appeared on his right flank at Æcae, on the edge of the Apulian plain. Hannibal at once offered battle, but neither by insults nor stratagems could he tempt or provoke Fabius to leave his safe position in the hills and risk a general engagement. The dictator clung fast to his policy of masterly inaction; by a warfare of outposts and skirmishes he trained his raw recruits and inexperienced officers, and restored their shaken confidence in Roman valour. Never

suffering himself to be brought to bay, yet constantly dogging the footsteps of the foe, the
cautious veteran cut off the Punic foragers, and
thus forced Hannibal to plunder the Italians,
whose aid he sought to win.　Disregarding the
rash suggestions of his lieutenant and the
murmurs of the camp, Fabius by his mere presence reassured the allies, and reduced the Punic
army to the verge of starvation.

The War
in Cam-
pania.

Hannibal, for whom striking success was a
necessity, soon resolved to transfer the war to
another theatre.　He had already tampered with
the fidelity of Capua, the second city of Italy,
ambitious of a yet higher place, and justly suspected by her jealous suzerain.　Even should his
hopes of her alliance be vain, he expected, by
wasting the richest lands in Italy, to force his
reluctant foe to fight, or, by proving the impot-
ence of Rome, to compel her allies to desert her
cause through fear if not through hate.　Eluding
the vigilance of Fabius, Hannibal passed through
the defiles of Samnium to Beneventum, and thence
marched northwards along the valley of the Calor
and Volturnus by Telesia to Allifæ.　Thence he
swooped down on the Falernian plain, the fairest
land in Italy, rich with corn and vines and
olives.　This fertile and beautiful region was ruth-
lessly pillaged by the Gauls and the Numidians,
who turned a garden into a desert.　The Roman
army, led by the mutinous master of the horse,

demanded instant battle. But Fabius paid no
heed to the idle clamours of the legions and of
the Roman mob. From the shelter of the Calli-
culan hills he watched, 'with stern contentment,'
the Punic army destroy the rich plunder of the
plain. He knew that Hannibal, without magazines, without a town in his possession, could not
winter where he was. He flattered himself with
the hope that by barring his retreat he might
catch him as in a pitfall. Hannibal was shut in
on every side—on the west by the sea, on the
south by the Volturnus, a broad and deep stream
which could only be crossed by the bridge at
Casilinum, now a Roman fortress held by a strong
garrison. The exits to the north by the Appian
and Latin roads Fabius had securely blocked by
holding the passes of Lautulæ and Suessa, and
the important position of Cales. The only line
of retreat was towards Allifæ by a narrow passage
between the river Volturnus and the hills, and
this opening Fabius guarded with 4000 picked
troops. His main army was stationed on the
neighbouring heights, ready to fall on the flank
of the retreating Carthaginians.

Hannibal was now in great straits. Laden as Stratagem
he was with prisoners booty and cattle, he could of Hanni-
not hope to force the pass without serious, per- bal.
haps disastrous, loss. He extricated himself by
a characteristic stratagem, in which he turned to
his own purpose the caution of Fabius, as he had

before utilised the rashness of a Flam
Sempronius. He chose from the vast 1
oxen in his camp some 2000 of the st
and bade his men fasten faggots of dry
wood on their horns. About two hours
midnight he ordered the faggots to be ligh
the oxen driven up into the hills. Madder
pain, the frightened beasts scoured the hill
the pass. There seemed all the signs of an army
in full retreat—a sound of trampling and the blaz-
ing fires of many torches. Completely deceived,
the Roman detachment moved away from the
pass to meet the fancied foe on the hills, while
Fabius, fearing an ambush, kept close within his
camp. When morning broke, the dictator found
that the whole Carthaginian army had marched
quietly through the unguarded pass, while his own
picked troops, panic-stricken by the strange noises,
the glare and the confusion of their night encounter, were now engaged with the light troops
of the Punic rear - guard. Finally Hannibal's
Spanish veterans drove them down into the plain,
and disappeared over the hills on their way to
rejoin their leader. Hannibal marched quietly
through Samnium, plundered the rich country of
the Pæligni, and finally returned to his old quarters
in Apulia. Still disappointed of Italian support,
he seized the little town of Gerunium on the edge
of the plain near Larinum, stocking it with corn
gathered from the surrounding country by his

active foragers, and forming a fortified camp in
front of the town. Fabius, true to his system,
followed in the tracks of the Punic army, and
encamped on the neighbouring hills.

But the signal failure of the unwelcome de- Fabius
and Minu-
fensive system rendered the dictator contemptible cius.
in the eyes of the people and the army. 'Hannibal's lackey' was condemned as a dotard enfeebled
by old age, or a traitor sold to the enemy. The
latter delusion Hannibal craftily fostered by spar-
ing the farms of Fabius, while he wasted the lands
round them with fire and sword. The discontent
came to a head during a short visit of the dictator
to Rome. He had strictly charged his lieutenant
not to risk a battle in his absence. The master
of the horse disobeyed his orders, but conducted
his operations with skill and success. He moved
his camp to a ridge of hills just above the plain,
and, without allowing himself to be drawn into
a pitched battle, checked the ravages of the
Numidians. Hannibal, to whom supplies for
the winter were absolutely necessary, had to
detach two - thirds of his force as foragers.
Minucius, seizing his opportunity, cut off a large
number of these scattered parties and advanced
in full array to attack the weak force left in the
Carthaginian camp. Hannibal had some difficulty
in holding his entrenchments till 4000 foragers,
rallied at the town of Gerunium, came to his
rescue. This spirited skirmish, which compelled

Hannibal to concentrate his forces close to
Gerunium, was magnified by rumour into a
decisive victory. The people, overjoyed at their
first success, and led on by the demagogues, M.
Metilius and C. Terentius Varro, appointed Minucius a colleague of the dictator, with equal powers.
But the folly of thus rewarding insubordination
and destroying the unity of the command was
soon made evident. Fabius, seeing that his new
colleague was bent on fighting, preferred to divide
the army rather than share the command. The
Roman generals now made their divisions patent
by occupying separate camps. Hannibal at once
resolved to draw Minucius into action. With a
force whose weakness invited attack, he occupied
a hill in front of his enemy's camp, but hard by,
in the hollows of the rolling ground, he had concealed some 5000 footmen and 500 Numidians,
with orders to fall on the enemy's rear in the
midst of the battle. Minucius rushed headlong
into the snare, and while hotly engaged in an
assault on the hill, was attacked in flank and rear by
the ambuscade. The retreat must soon have ended
in a rout like that of the Trebia, had not Fabius
come to the rescue and checked the Carthaginian
pursuit. Minucius frankly acknowledged his error,
and, surrendering his separate command, placed
himself once more under the orders of Fabius.
The rest of the campaign was quiet and uneventful, for, when after six months the dictator resigned

his office, the consuls, Cn. Servilius and M. Atilius Regulus, adhered steadily to the tactics of Fabius. The close of the year left Hannibal unconquered in the field, yet master only of the ground held by his army, as far as ever from the goal of his hopes. The Italian confederacy remained unbroken. Macedon still held back. Not a man had joined his standards except the brave but inconstant Celts. From Spain no reinforcements could be looked for while the Scipios kept Hasdrubal fully employed. From Carthage no substantial aid was forthcoming. The Roman Senate showed its stern courage in adversity by refusing the gifts of money offered by loyal allies, Pæstum and Neapolis, by warning Illyria and Macedon to keep quiet, and by the despatch of reinforcements to Spain.

Unfortunately, at a crisis when unity was necessary for the safety of the commonwealth, severe party struggles rent the Roman State. The mass of the people, impatient of constant military service, charged the Senate with the prolongation of the war, and threw on the government the odium of the dilatory strategy of Fabius. In opposition to the new nobility there was growing up a genuinely democratic party, which demanded the election of a true son of the people to the consulship, and a striking victory to maintain the supremacy of Rome. C. Terentius Varro, the son of a butcher, an eloquent demagogue and

Party Struggles at Rome.

bitter censor of the aristocratic party, had been
the chief supporter of the measure which gave
Minucius equal power with Fabius. His previous
career in office, and his regular employment even
after the disaster of Cannæ, attest his respectable
talents and character. But at such a crisis the
election of a mere civilian, destitute of military
skill and experience, was a signal example of the
inadequacy of Rome's municipal institutions for
an imperial and military policy. As if annual
election and divided leadership were not in
themselves enough, there was now to be added
the conduct of the war in a partisan spirit, the
repetition on a greater scale of the error which
had already cost Rome dear on the Trebia and
by Lake Trasimene. But Varro had the ear of the
people, discontented with the Senate's government,
and was returned alone as consul, no other
candidate obtaining a sufficient vote to entitle
him to election. It is creditable to him that, as
president at the comitia held to elect his colleague,
he used his influence in favour of L. Æmilius
Paullus, a good officer of the ordinary Roman
type, whose Illyrian victories had only brought
him unpopularity, since he was suspected of mal-
administration of the booty.

The Cam-
paign of
216 B.C.
　　Yet, though there was strife and division
between Senate and people, and even between
the two consuls, in one point all were agreed.
Hannibal was to be crushed at once by an over-

whelming force. The consuls had definite orders to offer battle, and were given the largest army that had ever been raised at Rome. Though still weak in cavalry, having but 6000 troopers to meet the 10,000 horsemen of Hannibal the consuls were well supplied with slingers archers and other light troops, and in infantry of the line they were twice as strong as the enemy. With eight strong Roman legions and a similar force of Italians, amounting in all to 80,000 footmen, they intended to sweep away the 40,000 Punic infantry. Hannibal, whose motley host had grown somewhat impatient of the cold and privations endured in their tedious winter quarters, welcomed the arrival of spring and the chance of battle. Successfully eluding the vigilance of the proconsuls, he broke up from Gerunium and surprised the Roman magazines in the fortified town of Cannæ. The consuls now arrived to assume the command and to bring the struggle to an issue.* By the seizure of Cannæ, Hannibal cut off the supplies and compelled the consuls either to give battle on a plain favourable to the Punic cavalry, or to surrender to the enemy the open country and the

---

* It would seem from the account in Polybius that the consuls did not reach the Roman camp till Hannibal had left Gerunium. If so, the stories in Livy of the apparently deserted camp, rich in plunder, with which he attempted to lure Varro to destruction, and the ingenious device which made Æmilius Paullus suspect a similar trap when Hannibal really broke up from Gerunium and marched on Cannæ, must be dismissed as inventions or exaggerations of the Roman annalist.

ripening harvest. The cautious Æmilius Paullus
would gladly have drawn the Carthaginian from
his favourable position, but Varro was bent on
instant battle. As the old foolish custom that
the consuls should command on alternate days
still prevailed at Rome, the rasher consul could
hurry his more prudent colleague into a position
in which there was no possibility of evading a
decisive contest.

The Battle-
field of
Cannæ.
In two days the Romans reached the river
Aufidus at a point about six miles above Hannibal's camp, which lay on the northern slope of
the hill of Cannæ, sheltered by the town from
the south-east wind. The consuls did not cross
the Aufidus, but pitched their camp on the left
bank. The course of the stream is, roughly
speaking, from south-east to north-west. The
Aufidus (Ofanto) is a mountain torrent, which,
though liable to heavy floods, has but a feeble
stream in the droughts of summer. Till within
eight miles of the sea it flows in a deep and
constant channel through a valley about a mile
in width, bounded by low hills of moderate
steepness. Below this point the river follows
a devious and shifting course till within two
miles of the sea, but neither its upper valley
nor any of its many bends allow space for the
manœuvres of large armies. In the eight miles
between the upper valley and the sea, the character of the country on the two banks of the

Aufidus differs. On the left stretches a vast plain almost on a level with the river, on the right there is a tract of gently undulating grassland separated from the plain beneath by a sharp rise in the ground. This shelving bank limits the vagaries of the river, which in ancient times seems to have flowed at its foot. The slope of ninety or a hundred feet, though steep enough to limit the field of battle, is hardly ever precipitous, and there are frequent gaps in it, up which cavalry could ride. In short, though not a dead level like the plain on the opposite side of the Aufidus, this undulating country is a thoroughly good piece of open fighting ground, and excellent for the movements of cavalry. Here Varro was more ready to risk a battle, nor was there the smallest reason why Hannibal should shrink from the contest. Elated by a successful skirmish, Varro had pitched his camp a mile below the Punic position on the opposite side of the Aufidus. Next day Æmilius Paullus, by occupying a smaller entrenchment on the right bank of the river, as well as the large camp on the left, endeavoured to restrict the enemy's supplies, and thus compel him to retire to a position less dangerous for infantry. In reply, Hannibal moved his camp to the left bank of the Aufidus, and after resting his troops for a day, offered Æmilius battle. When he found the more prudent consul resolved not to fight on such ground, he provoked Varro to fury by sending his Numidians across the stream to drive in the Roman watering parties, and pursue them to the very gates of the lesser camp.

Position of the Armies at Cannæ. At daybreak next morning, the red ensign—the well-known signal for battle—was seen flying above Varro's tent. The supposed advantages of the rolling ground on the right bank tempted the inexperienced general to cross the river and fight with his back to the sea, careless of retreat. Leaving 10,000 men to hold his larger camp, and to withdraw a division from the weak Carthaginian infantry by threatening their lines, he massed the legions in deep columns, covering their front with the light troops, the right flank with the weak Roman cavalry, and the left with the Italian horse.

They formed an imposing spectacle as they stood waiting eagerly for the expected fray. The sun on their left lit up a forest of waving plumes and shone on their brazen helmets. But the tactics of their leader were no better than his strategy had been. The wind, blowing strongly from the south, carried clouds of dust full in their faces, the cavalry on the right was hampered rather than protected by the stream, while the left wing was exposed on the open plain to the superior cavalry of the enemy. Above all, the legions, the real strength of the Roman army, were by an unusual and faulty disposition massed in dense columns. The gaps between the maniples were almost closed, and each maniple had a depth many times greater than its front. The result was that each legion formed a phalanx or column of cohorts, instead of the familiar triple line.

This extraordinary formation, which may have been forced on the Roman generals by the demoralisation of their troops, or the number of recruits in their ranks, sacrificed the advantage of superior numbers, and was a prime cause of the impending disaster. The lengthening of the files and shortening of the ranks may have been good tactics when, as in the first Punic war, elephants were to be encountered; it was fatal to offer a long flank to the attack of Hannibal's redoubtable cavalry. The blunder enabled Hannibal to show an equal front to the legions. Throwing forward his Gallic and Spanish infantry in a crescent - like formation, he stationed his African veterans, now re-armed in Roman fashion, in deep narrow columns at either end of the crescent. The heavy cavalry was posted near the river on the left, the Numidians on the right were led by Hanno and Maharbal, the slingers and light troops covered the whole line. Hannibal himself, with his brother Mago, took command of the centre. His camp was on the other side of the Aufidus; the strong town of Canusium, scarcely five miles off, threatened his rear, so that defeat must have meant destruction. But as he looked

F

on the wide plain around, on his veteran infantry and matchless horsemen, he felt assured of victory. When one of his officers named Gisgo remarked on the astonishing number of the Roman host, he rallied him on having forgotten the yet more astonishing fact that not one among them was called Gisgo, and the laugh that followed satisfied his soldiers of their general's confidence.

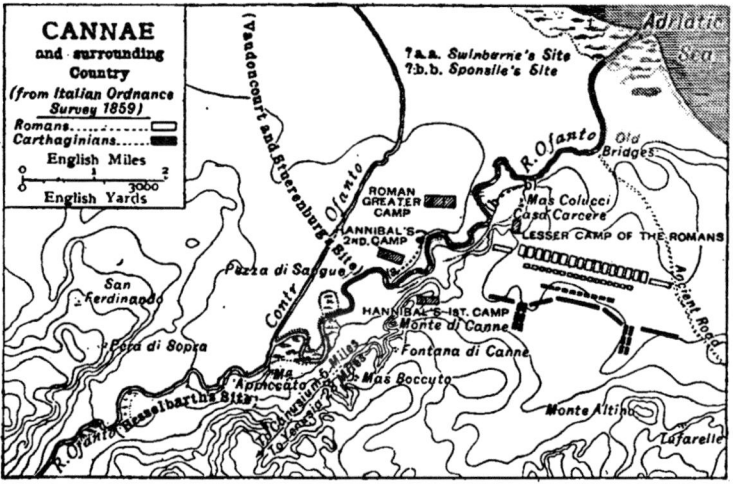

Battle of Cannæ. The battle began with the usual indecisive skirmishing between the light armed troops. Then Hasdrubal and his heavy horsemen swept down on the inferior Roman cavalry under Æmilius Paullus. Packed closely in a narrow space, the two bodies met front to front in deadly conflict. Many of the troopers leaped from their horses and fought man to man on foot. But in the end the outnumbered Romans were totally routed and driven off the field. Hasdrubal chased them before him along the river, but soon recalled his squadrons, and rode off to the left wing, where he found the Numidians skirmishing with the Italian horsemen led by Varro. They broke and fled before his approaching squadrons, and Hasdrubal, wisely leaving pursuit and slaughter to the swift and unsparing Numidians, crowned his signal services by an irresistible charge upon the rear of the Roman infantry.

The Roman legions under Servilius, finding the Gauls and Spaniards advancing against them in a convex line, pressed forward with a converging front till the whole army became one huge column. By sheer weight of numbers it broke through the Gallic and Spanish ranks, and like the English foot at Fontenoy, advanced victorious into the heart of the enemy's position. But while the head of the column was still engaged with the Gauls and Spaniards, the Libyans, facing right and left, fell upon its flanks, and Hasdrubal's victorious horsemen charged with thundering fury upon its rear. The doomed legions still fought stoutly for life, if not for victory. But only one end was possible to such a struggle. Attacked on all sides, crowded together in hopeless confusion, the Roman soldiery fell where they stood, unable either to fight or fly. The lost battle ended in a hideous and general butchery, till night enabled the poor remains of that gallant host to escape under cover of darkness. The consul Æmilius Paullus, his predecessor Servilius, the late master of the horse Minucius, and eighty senators lay dead upon the field. Varro, with seventy horsemen, had fled for safety to Venusia.

The Roman army was wiped off the face of the earth, and for their total destruction Hannibal had sacrificed but 6000 men. The victory was followed by the capture of the two camps, and the surrender of the troops which held them. At least 50,000 men had fallen, some 20,000 were captured on the field or in the camps ; not more than 10,000 escaped. The fugitives made their way through the broken ranks of the Spaniards and Gauls to Canusium, where they were joined by the braver spirits from the two camps, and the surviving consul.

With the victory of Cannæ the second act in the drama of the Hannibalic war closes. Hitherto the course of the hero has been one long succession of triumphs ; hereafter, though still invincible in the field, he is thwarted and baffled by the weakness and irresolution of his countrymen and allies, and by the iron will of the Roman aristocracy. After the splendour of the opening years comes the long tragedy of hope deferred and failing strength, till Hannibal is left, like Hector, alone to fight the battle of an ungrateful city, and falls, like Hector, before a rival stronger but less noble.

CHAPTER V

THE WAR FROM CANNÆ TO THE FALL OF CAPUA

'FROM New Carthage to the plains of Cannæ,' Change in the Character of the War. as has been well said by Dr Arnold, 'Hannibal's march resembles a mighty torrent, which rushing along irresistible and undivided, fixes our attention to the one line of its course,' shutting out all other sights. 'But from Cannæ onwards the character of the scene changes.' The theatre of the war is widened, the action takes place in so many different countries, in Spain, Sicily, Sardinia, and Macedon, that not only dramatic unity but even historic interest suffers; the personality of the hero, though as truly as ever the moving and directing power in all that befell, does not so obviously dominate the scene. The nation gradually rises above the individual; Rome meets with unshaken front the fierce assaults of many foes, she gains time and space to breathe by rapid blows which disable her smaller enemies abroad, while she slowly unfastens from her own throat the deadly grip of her chief antagonist.

Rome had been a ¡prey to the most intense Rome after Cannæ. anxiety as the day of Cannæ drew near. Every temple and every altar was besieged by clamorous supplicants. When the fatal tidings arrived, no pen can picture the grief and terror of a stricken people. Every household without exception had to mourn its dead; yet after the first moments of panic, order was completely restored. Q. Fabius Maximus, though not in office, guided the counsels of the Senate with piety, wisdom, and courage. The general mourning was cut short; with the enemy at the gates it was no time to give way to lamentation. The walls were manned, the forum cleared, and the assemblies of the people suspended. A solemn embassy was sent to Delphi, and if, as at the crisis of the Gallic war, human sacrifices were offered to the offended gods, this was the only token that despair had infected the faith of Rome. Nor were human precautions neglected. A tried and trusted veteran, M. Claudius Marcellus, was ordered to lead a legion of marines from Ostia to Apulia, and to take command of the forces there collected. In the camp as in the city, the spirit of discipline triumphed over panic. A plot among some of the younger nobles, headed by a degenerate Metellus, to fly beyond sea and seek some foreign service, was repressed by the energy and firmness of young P. Scipio. Varro from the wreck of his army formed two weak legions. At the bidding of the Senate he promptly handed them over to Marcellus, and himself returned home to face the obloquy and punishment which might well await the general, who had fled from the ruin wrought by his own recklessness. But the senators showed that in the hour of need they could rise above the spirit of faction. A Punic commander, who had survived such a disaster, would have paid the penalty on the cross; the Roman was awarded the thanks of the Senate, because he had not despaired of the republic. Yet this ceremony was neither an elaborate mockery of a discredited opponent, nor a hypocritical concealment of bitter resentment under a sounding phrase; it was a real reconciliation between the people and the aristocracy.

Hannibal was not idle after Cannæ. True, he would not sanction the rush on Rome proposed by Maharbal on the field of battle, quietly ignoring the taunt of that hot-headed cavalry officer that he could gain but not follow up a victory. Even Napoleon supposed that Hannibal might have ended the war by an advance, such as he himself so often made, on the enemy's capital. But though in modern warfare the fate of nations is decided on the field of battle, in ancient times, when the system of defence was far superior to the means of attack, often a victorous army was shattered in a vain assault on the strong walls of a fortified town. It was equally impossible to surprise, to storm or to blockade Rome. Hannibal had but 45,000 tired men under his command, he was without a siege train, he must have made a

Hannibal refuses to march on Rome.

long and difficult march through a hostile country,
and he could not afford to fail. The defeat of
Regulus before Carthage showed how the real
fruits of the most brilliant victory might be lost, if
time were wasted in an empty demonstration.

Capua and
South
Italy join
Hannibal.
 Hannibal intended to assail not the city, but the
confederacy. For there were at last signs that
the solid fabric of the Italian alliance was breaking down under the intolerable strain. All the
Bruttians, except the men of Petelia and Consentia, and the majority of the Lucanians, passed
over to his side. The Samnite tribes except the
Pentrians, and of the Apulian towns Arpi, Salapia
and Herdonea, joined in the revolt. Last and
most important of all was the defection of Capua,
the second city of Italy, capable of raising an army
of 30,000 foot and 4000 horsemen. There, as in
most Italian cities, the aristocracy, who in this case
possessed the full Roman franchise and owed their
wealth and power in part to the good will of the
Senate, remained true to Rome. But the people,
though they shared the private rights of Roman
burgesses, and actually served in a special legion
by their side, while they retained local autonomy
under their own Senate and magistrate (*Meddix
Tuticus*), were jealous of Roman superiority, and
exasperated by the loss of their public land. The
weak and unpopular Senate, intimidated by an
ambitious noble, Pacuvius Calavius, yielded to the
clamour of the people, and concluded a treaty with

Hannibal, which guaranteed to the Capuans entire independence, and in particular, immunity from military service and other burthens. The treaty was sealed by the murder of the Roman residents in Capua, an act of treachery which placed the city beyond the reach of forgiveness. But the true value of the liberty which had just been solemnly guaranteed, and of the hope that by Punic aid Capua might become mistress of Italy, was soon made unpleasantly clear by the fate of the aristocratic leader Decius Magius, whose obstinate adherence to the cause of Rome and defiance of Hannibal were punished by arrest and deportation at the command of the Carthaginian.

Meanwhile in Rome extraordinary efforts were made to organise a force capable of taking the field. M. Junius Pera was made dictator, and Ti. Sempronius Gracchus master of the horse. The dictator enlisted 8000 slaves purchased by the State, and armed with the spoils of former wars taken down from the temples. He offered pardon to criminals and release to debtors if they would now take arms. Mere boys and old men bowed with age were enrolled for the defence of the city. But there was one marked exception to this general levy. Hannibal was ready enough to treat for the release of his Roman prisoners.* *Measures to raise Troops.*

---

* The story that Hannibal vented his rage on these unfortunate prisoners with inhuman cruelty is utterly discredited by the silence of the best authorities, Polybius and Livy.

But the Senate absolutely forbade the payment of a ransom, neither choosing to provide Hannibal with funds, nor to rescue from slavery men who had allowed themselves to be taken alive. Rome must teach her soldiers that it was better to die than surrender. As a sign of their fixed determination to carry on this war to the death, the Senate rejected Hannibal's offer, and dismissed his envoy Carthalo without listening for a moment to a proposal for peace.

Marcellus and Hannibal in Campania. The war now centred in Campania. After Cannæ Hannibal moved on Compsa in Samnium, which he used as a depôt for his baggage and plunder. He ordered Mago to receive the submission of Bruttium, and thence take ship for Carthage to bear thither the news of Cannæ. Hannibal further detached Hanno to Lucania, and marched himself with his main army on Capua. The revolt of that city, which was imitated by two neighbouring towns, Atella and Calatia, drew the Roman forces to Campania. The dictator took post at Teanum, on the northern edge of the Falernian plain, while Marcellus pushed forward to Casilinum, but found it already too late to save Capua. Neapolis and Cumæ, Greek cities whose harbours would have been of great value to Hannibal, courageously repelled the assaults of the hated Phœnician. At Nola, as at Capua, the common people were ready to open the gates to the invader, had not Marcellus received timely warning from the nobles. Marching round by the hills, he descended suddenly on the disaffected city, and terrified the popular party by some bloody executions. When Hannibal approached to take possession of the place, Marcellus sallied boldly forth and repulsed him with some loss. This slight check was magnified by Roman annalists into a serious defeat, but sober history can only allow Marcellus credit for his courage in daring to face Hannibal at a time when not to be conquered by him was more difficult than it was afterwards to conquer him. Having done good service in restoring the morale of his troops, Marcellus retired to his camp above Suessula. Hannibal, notwithstanding his failure at Nola, conquered Nuceria and Acerræ in the same neighbourhood, and laid siege to Casilinum, an important fortress commanding the bridge over the Volturnus, at the junction of the Appian and Latin roads. The garrison, composed of two allied cohorts from Perusia and Præneste, made a desperate resistance, which obliged Hannibal to turn the siege into a blockade. Towards the end of the winter, famine compelled these valiant Italians to yield, on condition that they were allowed to ransom themselves. Their obstinate defence was of very good omen for the cause of Rome.

During the blockade of Casilinum, Hannibal sent the bulk of his forces into winter quarters at Hannibal's Difficulties

Capua (216 B.C.). It may be that their discipline suffered amid the pleasures of the town, but only the distorted vision of a rhetorical moralist would see in this indulgence the ruin of an army, or find in Capua Hannibal's Cannæ. Hannibal's army remained as formidable as ever in the field; the true reasons for the change in the fortunes of the war are to be found, not in the demoralisation of his troops, but in their scanty numbers, in the lack of engineers and of artillery, in the improved strategy of the Roman commanders. Hannibal was no doubt in military possession of Italy south of the Volturnus, with Capua as his base, but it was already evident that his Italian allies were as much of a burden as of a blessing. Only the Lucanians and Bruttians gave him any considerable support, and even in those regions Petelia and Consentia prolonged for a year (216-5 B.C.) a forlorn defence. Of the Greek cities, Locri and Croton capitulated unwillingly to a superior force of Bruttians and Carthaginians, but Rhegium, Thurii, Tarentum and Metapontum still held out. The Latin colonies, such as Brundisium, Venusia, Luceria, Æsernia, Beneventum, Pæstum and Cales were firmly knit to Rome by the double bond of honour and of interest. The colonists were like Cromwell's Ironsides settled in Ireland, a garrison in a foreign land, at feud with the natives whose land they held. These fortresses hampered Hannibal's movements in the field and menaced his communications. The war seemed likely to turn into a series of sieges, in which Hannibal's strongest arm, his cavalry, was useless. The Campanians and Apulians were lukewarm in the Punic cause, and proved rather a hindrance than a help. In fine, Hannibal found himself too weak at once to mask the Roman fortresses, to defend his allies, and to resume the offensive. But Hannibal had always regarded his own army as the mere vanguard of a mighty host that was to be gathered against Rome from all the earth. He looked to his countrymen in Carthage and in Spain, and to the court of Macedon, to finish the work so splendidly begun. He sowed the seeds of sedition in Sicily, in Sardinia, and Cisalpine Gaul, that Rome might reap a bitter harvest for past injustice. His plans were wrecked by the suicidal folly of the Gaul and the Macedonian, by the failure of the Punic government to grasp the true nature of the struggle in which it was involved, and by the skill and energy with which the Roman Senate, by operations in Spain and Greece, isolated their great opponent in South Italy.

It is therefore necessary briefly to survey the progress of events beyond the borders of Italy during the triumphant progress of Hannibal from the Ebro to Capua. In Cisalpine Gaul a fearful disaster had befallen the Roman arms. L. Postumius Albinus, who had been sent as prætor

The War in Cisalpine Gaul.

(216 B.C.) with two legions to keep the unruly tribes in check, and was elected consul for the ensuing year, before he could assume the consulship fell into a Gallic ambush in the Silva Litana, and was cut to pieces with his whole force. His skull set in gold was used by the barbarians as a goblet at solemn banquets, a ghastly trophy of a signal triumph. But the Gauls made no use of their victory. Though Rome, too weak to avenge her defeat, contented herself with posting an army of observation under Pomponius Matho at Ariminum, with a legion in reserve under Varro in Picenum, no host of the clans poured into Italy, or even troubled Placentia and Cremona. No Punic officer was there to organise the attack ; the more active and vigorous of the clansmen were already fighting under Hannibal's banner ; possibly the short-sighted barbarians were well content to let the Carthaginian fight their battles. Whatever may have been the reason, Celtic inaction allowed Rome to use the resources of Etruria and Umbria for the maintenance of the war in South Italy.

The Scipios in Spain.
Yet more important was the course of the war in Spain. In 218 B.C. Cn. Scipio had landed at Emporiæ in command of his brother's legions, and had soon stirred up the Catalans to revolt from Carthage. A defeat at Cissis, in which Hanno was made prisoner, drove the Carthaginians beyond the Ebro. Scipio established himself firmly at Tarraco, and held his ground against

the forces of Hasdrubal. Next year the Roman
army was strengthened by the arrival of another
legion under P. Scipio, yet less was effected by
open force than by stratagem and diplomacy. Cn.
Scipio surprised and annihilated the Carthaginian
fleet at the mouth of the Ebro, and the brothers
won golden opinions throughout the Peninsula by
restoring to their friends the Spanish hostages
whom the treachery of Abelux, and the guileless
simplicity of the Carthaginian commandant at
Saguntum, had placed in their hands. Hasdrubal
dare not trust his Spanish levies to encounter the
popular and victorious Romans. He stamped out
(B.C. 216) a revolt in the valley of the Baetis, and
after receiving some urgently needed reinforcements from Carthage, attempted to follow in
Hannibal's footsteps across the Pyrenees. But
he had not force enough to open the way to Italy
and come to the aid of his brother. The Scipios
met him near Ibera on the Ebro, and owing to the
treachery or cowardice of his Spanish conscripts,
defeated and dispersed his army. This great
victory, followed next year (215 B.C.) by further
successes in the heart of Andalusia at Intibili
and Illiturgi, deprived Hannibal of all hope of
reinforcements from Spain, and preserved Rome
from a double attack which might well have
proved fatal to her very existence. The victories
of the Scipios in Spain not only crippled Hasdrubal, but further diverted the reinforcements

expected by Hannibal from Carthage. In the
first flush of triumph after Cannæ, the voice
of opposition was silenced. Mago, who bore to
Carthage the despatches of Hannibal, poured out
on the floor of the Carthaginian Senate House a
bushel of gold rings taken from the fingers of the
Roman knights who fell at Cannæ. Moved by the
sight, the Senate resolved to raise a large force in
Spain, and send forthwith to Hannibal's aid 4000
Numidians and 40 elephants. But the defeat
of Hasdrubal proved the untrustworthiness of
Spanish conscripts, and the urgent need of succour
from Africa. Eventually Mago was sent with the
bulk of the forces to Spain ; only the elephants
and cavalry reached Hannibal in Italy.

Macedon, Sicily and Sardinia.
        Notwithstanding these misfortunes, the year 215
B.C. seemed bright with promise for Hannibal.
Philip of Macedon, egged on by Demetrius of
Pharos, resolved to purchase Punic support in his
Greek wars, and the reversion of the Roman
possessions in Illyria, by throwing his weight into
the scale of Carthage. His ambassadors concluded an offensive and defensive alliance with
Hannibal. In the same year the half subdued
natives of Sardinia were driven by the requisitions
of the starving Roman garrisons into open
rebellion. But the gravest loss of all to the
Roman cause was the death of their true ally, the
sage and discreet ruler of Syracuse. For fifty-four
years Hiero had secured for his subjects prosperity

and honour. For nearly fifty he had preserved his alliance with Rome without forfeiting his independence or incurring the ill will of Carthage. His object had been to develop the resources of his kingdom, and promote the progress of the arts and sciences at home, while abroad he sought safety in the mutual fears of the two great powers, and in the sure alliance of Rome. This cautious and sagacious policy was reversed by his young and ambitious grandson, Hieronymus, who welcomed to his court the dexterous emissaries of Hannibal, Hippocrates and Epicydes, apt pupils of their master in military and political intrigue, and at their instigation repudiated the Roman and joined the Carthaginian alliance. Yet the performance of the year did not fulfil its early promise. The capture of the Macedonian ambassadors as they were returning home compelled Philip to send a second embassy, and prolonged his inaction for another year. The loss of time and opportunity proved irreparable, since Rome, thus warned of the king's intentions, took prompt and decisive action. Within a year M. Valerius Lævinus sailed across the Adriatic to form a Greek coalition against Macedon (214 B.C.). The Sardinian revolt was utterly quelled. The ample succours despatched by Carthage under Hasdrubal Calvus were delayed by tempests ; and the veteran T. Manlius Torquatus beat first the Sardinians and then the combined Punic and native armies.

He finally restored the absolute sovereignty of Rome by the reduction and punishment of the revolted towns, and leaving but a single legion behind, returned home to report the complete submission of the island (215 B.C.).

The War in Campania.

Not even in Italy, where he himself commanded, did Hannibal mark the year 215 B.C. with a victory. He lay quiet on Mount Tifata, above Capua, watching for an opportunity of striking a blow against the armies which encircled him, and waiting for the development of events in Spain Sicily and Macedon. Round him were gathered three Roman armies, over 60,000 strong in all. Fabius at Cales guarded the Latin road, Gracchus at Liternum protected the Greek harbours, and Marcellus from his mountain camp above Suessula watched the unstable Nolans. Gracchus opened the campaign with the surprise and massacre of 2000 Capuans who had come to celebrate a Campanian festival at Hamæ. He declared that the Capuans were caught in the snare that they had laid for the men of Cumæ, but the suspicion scarcely justifies his own treachery. Hannibal came too late to avenge his slaughtered allies, and failed in an attack on Cumæ. Meanwhile Fabius marched round Capua, covered by the hills, stormed the town of Saticula, and joined Marcellus above Suessula. That active officer was sent on to Nola, where the plots of the popular party still caused the Romans anxiety. In three days' skirmishing Marcellus gained some advantage over the Carthaginians, whose leader would appear to have been bent rather on effecting his junction with Bomilcar and the reinforcements from Carthage than on the capture of the town. Hannibal, baffled if not beaten, marched off to Apulia to check the forays of Lævinus, but already, after the defeat of his lieutenant Hanno at Grumentum, the Samnites and Lucanians were crying out for aid.

Taught by fearful experience, the Roman generals had now learned their lesson. They did not passively follow in Hannibal's track, leaving him to work his will unmolested, still less did they rush wildly on the enemy wherever they found him, but taking up strong positions under the walls of fortresses or entrenched camps, they only accepted battle where the chances were in their favour, and where defeat did not entail disaster. The improved conduct of the war by experienced generals retained in commands for a lengthened period rendered impossible those brilliant strokes of genius which marked the earlier career of Hannibal. Encouraged by the change in the fortune of the war, the Romans made great sacrifices in the hope that they might be fruitful of success. When doubled taxes proved inadequate to the needs of the State, and too burdensome to the taxpayer, a forced contribution was levied for the navy, amounting in

Skill and Energy of the Romans.

substance to a graduated property tax. An appeal to the patriotism of the monied classes by the prætor Q. Fulvius, to lend capital to the State without demanding interest, met with a ready answer. Three companies were formed to supply the corn and clothing required by the armies in Spain ; in return they required the government to grant them exemption from military service, and to guarantee them against all risks from storm or foe. The public spirit of the contractors was unhappily alloyed with an admixture of jobbery and dishonesty : some at least of their number were guilty of scuttling ships of small value, in order to recover a high rate of insurance from the government.

Campaign of 214 B.C.
By these great exertions twenty legions were kept on foot, as well as a fleet of 150 sail. Eight were to take the field against Hannibal and his lieutenants in Apulia Campania and Lucania; two were in reserve at Rome, the rest were watching Gaul and Macedon, or engaged in Spain Sicily and Sardinia. Summoned to the defence of Capua, Hannibal moved from Arpi to Mount Tifata. He was hemmed in by three Roman armies; one consul, old Q. Fabius, took command at Cales, the other, Marcellus, above Suessula, and now the pro-consul Gracchus advanced to Beneventum, his place at Luceria being taken by the prætor, young Q. Fabius. Hannibal, after a vain attempt to surprise Puteoli,

swept like a fiery flood from Mount Tifata to the shore of the Adriatic, laying waste the whole land. He had hoped that the men of Tarentum, who had invited his help, would have placed in his hands their excellent harbour, equally convenient for the reception of reinforcements from Carthage and of aid from Macedon. But three days before he came a Roman officer, M. Livius, had repressed the popular party, sent its leaders as hostages to Rome, and with the aid of the Tarentine aristocrats, manned the walls and garrisoned the citadel. Hannibal retired, baffled, to winter in Apulia. Meanwhile the Roman consuls utilised his absence to press the siege of Casilinum. The Capuan garrison, after an obstinate defence, agreed to surrender the town to Fabius in return for a safe conduct to Capua. But as they were marching out, Marcellus forced his way through the open gate into the town, and cut to pieces or captured the unhappy defenders. After this act of treachery Marcellus returned to Nola, where he fell ill, and Fabius ravaged Samnium. The chief honours of the campaign rested with the pro-consul Gracchus. At the head of his slave-legions he utterly routed the Lucanian and Bruttian levies of Hanno near Beneventum. With wise generosity Gracchus granted liberty to all his soldiers, whether they had behaved well in the action or not, and commemorated, by a picture placed in the temple of Liberty, not his own

victory, but the triumphant reception of the en-
franchised slaves at Beneventum. Hanno escaped
with his cavalry into Bruttium.

Campaign of 213 B.C.

The next campaign in Italy (213 B.C.) was also
uneventful. Fabius recovered Arpi by treachery,
and in Bruttium and Lucania the Romans won
some slight successes. But Hanno checked the
reaction in favour of Rome by dispersing some
irregular levies raised by T. Pomponius Veientanus.
Hannibal himself passed the whole summer near
Tarentum, loth to give up all hope of so great a
prize. By dint of great and exhausting efforts,
Rome fully held her ground. The system of warfare adopted by her generals was not brilliant,
and involved much waste of power and loss of
time, but it gradually wore down the strength of
Hannibal, and in spite of Punic success in Sicily,
turned the scale in favour of Rome.

Capture of Tarentum.

In the winter 213-212 B.C., Hannibal at last
achieved his purpose and captured Tarentum.
The cruel execution of the hostages held by Rome
for an attempt to escape from captivity proved
a blunder, if not a crime. Hannibal's partisans
felt themselves now free to act as their desire
for vengeance prompted them. Two young men,
Philemenus and Nicon, took the lead in a conspiracy to surrender the town to the Carthaginians,
and on pretence of hunting found means of seeing
Hannibal and concluding a treaty with him, in
which he bound himself to respect the liberties

of the town and the lives and properties of the citizens. The situation of the town favoured the designs of the conspirators. It forms a triangle, washed on two sides by water, on the west by the Mediterranean, on the north-east by the Mare Piccolo, a land-locked harbour with a narrow entrance. On a rocky knoll at the apex of the triangle stood the citadel, which was held by a Roman garrison, and commanded the mouth of the port. An assault by land was only possible on the south-eastern side, where the wall stretched across from sea to sea, forming the base of the triangle far away from the citadel. Here lay the burial ground of Tarentum, between the gates and the inhabited quarters of the town. In this lonely spot Nicon and some other conspirators waited for the promised fire-signal from Hannibal. As soon as they saw it, they rushed to the gate, put the guards to the sword, and admitted a troop of Gauls and Numidians into the town. At the same moment Philemenus, returning with three friends from the chase, gained admission by the postern of another gate, slew its guardian, and brought in thirty Africans. These mastered the gatehouse and towers, killed the guard, and opened the main gate to a column of Libyans. No alarm had yet reached the Roman garrison. Hannibal at once ordered his Gallic troops to occupy the chief streets leading to the market place, and to kill every Roman who fell in their way. The conspirators now blew on some Roman trumpets the well-known call to arms. Roused by the sound, the unhappy soldiers quartered in the town rushed into the snare. They were cut down by the Gauls as they poured into the streets. The commandant was more fortunate. Scarcely yet recovered from a debauch of the previous evening, he fled to the harbour and reached the citadel by boat. When morning dawned, Hannibal caused the citizens to be summoned to an assembly, and told them they had nothing to fear. He came to deliver them from the yoke of Rome, and would give up to plunder only the houses and property of Romans. All houses over whose door was written ' the house of a Tarentine' should be spared.

The Citadel holds out. Thus Tarentum was won, but the citadel still held out, and by its position threatened the town, and shut up the Tarentine fleet in the harbour. To repress the sallies of the garrison, Hannibal made a wall and ditch between the citadel and the town. When the Romans tried to interrupt his works, he lured them on by a pretended flight, and then turning suddenly on them, drove them in with great slaughter. Nevertheless reinforcements from Metapontum encouraged the garrison to make another sally, in which they destroyed Hannibal's siege-works, and compelled him to trust to a blockade. To gain the mastery of the sea, Hannibal contrived to drag the Tarentine ships through the streets, right across the tongue

of land on which the town lay, from the inner harbour to the open sea. But in spite of the block-
ading squadron, some bold merchantmen brought
a supply of corn to the beleaguered garrison.
The fall of Tarentum was a great blow to the
Roman arms. Thurii Metapontum and Heraclea
followed the example of the chief city in Magna
Græcia, and so opened the whole coast for the
expected coming of the Macedonian phalanx.
Yet Philip wasted his feverish energy on aim-
less enterprises, and sacrificed the chance of a
vigorous assertion of Hellenism in Italy to petty
and futile successes in border warfare.

The main scene of the struggle now shifts to Disorder
Sicily (214 B.C.). The childish vanity and cruel in Sicily.
suspicions of the young tyrant Hieronymus enabled the Roman party in Syracuse to contrive
his assassination in the narrow street of Leontini.
The conspirators won Syracuse for their cause by
raising the cry of liberty, but stained their triumph
by the treacherous murder of Andranodorus and
Themistius, kinsmen and counsellors of Hieronymus, who had nevertheless accepted office under
the new republic. A darker crime followed—the
proscription of five helpless women, all that was
left of the race of Hiero. In the reaction that
followed this ruthless crime, Hippocrates and
Epicydes were elected generals. Yet the aristocratic party, encouraged by the arrival of a strong
Roman fleet under the prætor Appius Claudius,

renewed the ancient alliance with Rome. But many of the cities which had belonged to the realm of Hiero refused to follow the lead of Syracuse. At Leontini, the head and centre of this revolt, Hippocrates and Epicydes found refuge. They were now the leaders of the popular party in Sicily, and were busily employed in spreading the insurrection against Rome.

Marcellus in Sicily.

While Syracuse, the Paris of antiquity, was thus torn by faction and shaken by revolution, Rome was making ready for a decisive blow. The 'ever-victorious' Marcellus had been ordered to Sicily in 214 B.C., but, delayed by sickness, seems not to have reached the island till the spring of the succeeding year. He at once fell on Leontini, stormed the town, and made sack and slaughter more terrible by the execution in cold blood of 2000 Roman deserters. The tidings roused a storm of indignation throughout Sicily, and enabled Hippocrates and his brother, who had fled to Herbessus, to excite mutiny among the mercenaries led by the Syracusan generals against them. Placing themselves at the head of the mutinous army, the two brothers marched on Syracuse, overpowered the resistance of the aristocrats, and set up a government favourable to democracy and Carthage. Massacre followed on the heels of revolution; slaves and prisoners were set free; the city mob and the foreign mercenaries controlled the destinies of Syracuse.

With fiery vehemence Marcellus hastened on
against the doomed city, and at once began the
siege by land and sea. Syracuse consisted of
three separate walled towns. The island of
Ortygia, the oldest settlement, had now become
the fortress arsenal and palace of the lords of
Syracuse. Along the coast ran the newer town
of Achradina, behind which there had grown up
two suburbs, Tyche and Neapolis. These had
been enclosed by the triangular lines of the elder
Dionysius, which crown the converging slopes of
Epipolæ, and are strengthened at their apex by
the elaborate fortress of Euryalus. These great
walls, eighteen miles in length, though but weakly
defended, might by their own strength have defied
the Roman assaults. They were further admirably
furnished with scientific engines of war by the
great mathematician Archimedes. Vainly Marcellus attempted by a discharge of missiles from
his ships to clear the sea-wall of Achradina of its
defenders, and so prepare the way for an escalade.
Showers of arrows from unseen enemies within
the loopholed wall decimated the helpless
assailants. Giant poles were thrust out from
the top of the walls, and great stones or
masses of lead dropped from them on their
scaling ladders; or huge cranes seized the ships
with iron grapples, raised them from the water,
and then dashed them down again with destruc-
tive violence. In despair Marcellus put a stop to

the assaults, and contented himself with a loose blockade.

To add to his difficulties, the stout resistance of Syracuse now kindled the spirit of revolt in other Sicilian cities. Many deeds of cruelty, which culminated in the treacherous massacre of the citizens of Enna by the Roman garrison, added fuel to the flame. Carthage herself, more eager to regain her ancient possessions in Sicily than to support the greatest of her sons in Italy, had sent a large fleet and army to help the insurgents. Himilco, after reducing Agrigentum, marched on Syracuse, and was joined by Hippocrates, who broke through the Roman army. Marcellus, after a vain attempt to stem the tide of Sicilian revolt, fell back on his lines before Syracuse. The Punic host lay encamped on the banks of the Anapus, and a fleet under Bomilcar entered the harbour. Where force had failed, treachery and carelessness proved themselves useful allies to Rome. During the three days' festival of Artemis, while the whole city was given over to revelling and drunkenness, the Roman soldiers scaled a weak place in the unguarded walls. Guided by the traitor Sosis, they seized the strongly fortified gate, Hexapylon, the key of the northern wall of Epipolæ. Marcellus from the high ground looked down on Achradina and Ortygia. The surrender of the great castle of Euryalus by its governor secured his position, while the plunder of Tyche and Neapolis whetted the appetite of the legions for the yet richer spoils of the still uncaptured quarters of the town.

Meanwhile, the defenders of Syracuse were not inactive. Epicydes summoned to her help the additional forces which Hippocrates and Himilco had assembled. While the combined Carthaginian and Sicilian armies assaulted the camp of Crispinus near the Olympieum on the rising ground beyond the Anapus, Epicydes himself sallied forth from Achradina to assail Marcellus. But Roman legionaries behind fortifications were invincible, and as summer advanced the malarial fevers, which had more than once destroyed the enemies of Syracuse, now wrought havoc in the hosts encamped by the marshes for her defence. Hippocrates and Himilco perished with the bulk of the Carthaginian forces, and the Sicilians dispersed to their homes. Meanwhile, the Roman soldiers quartered in the houses on the high ground suffered but little, while famine, disease and anarchy reigned in the distracted city. Epicydes slipped away; the fleet of Bomilcar, detained by contrary winds, failed to bring the expected relief. The Roman deserters and the mercenaries triumphed over the native Syracusans, and established a reign of terror only ended by the betrayal of the city to Marcellus. A Spanish captain named Mericus secretly admitted a small party of Romans into Ortygia; next morning, under

Fall of Syracuse. 212 B.C.

cover of a general assault on the land front
of Achradina, more legionaries landed from
boats, and gained possession of the whole island.
Achradina, now defenceless, was handed over by
Marcellus to plunder and rapine. Amidst the
horrors and tumult of the sack, Archimedes,
whom even the ruthless Marcellus would gladly
have spared, was slain by a common soldier.
Syracuse fell to rise no more to greatness or to
liberty. Stripped of its works of· art, the enslaved
city was driven by a hard fate to extol the tender
mercies of the rough soldier, who set an example
of high-handed robbery only too faithfully copied
by later conquerors.

Capua.   The capture of Syracuse was followed by a yet
greater triumph for Rome—the fall of Capua.
Early in the spring of 212 B.C., the Romans
had resolved to besiege the town. The two
new consuls, the veteran Q. Fulvius Flaccus and
Appius Claudius, marching from Apulia and
Campania, united their forces at Bovianum, ready
to advance on Capua. Gracchus was still stationed
in Lucania, the prætor C. Nero was ordered to
take command of the camp above Suessula. Thus
there were at least ten legions to assail Capua
and confront Hannibal, should he come to its
relief. The Carthaginian leader was still fully
occupied at Tarentum, but in response to the
urgent entreaties of the Capuans, he directed
Hanno to move on Beneventum and throw

supplies into the threatened town. Hanno, marching from Lucania with a speed which surprised
both friend and foe, reached the neighbourhood
of Beneventum in safety. The negligence and
apathy of the Capuans ruined a bold and judicious
scheme.   Hanno rapidly collected in his camp
an abundant supply of corn, but their transport
was not ready to take it to Capua. News was
sent to the consuls at Bovianum of Hanno's
perilous situation, and by a night march and
sudden sally from Beneventum, Fulvius routed
the Punic army, stormed the camp, and captured
the whole convoy. Hanno, with the wreck of his
army, beat a hasty retreat.

In response to another appeal for aid from the Attempts
unworthy Capuans, Hannibal, who could not yet Capua.
to relieve
leave Magna Græcia, sent them 2000 of his
invincible horsemen. The consuls, as they closed
in upon the town, summoned Gracchus from
Lucania to cover the siege. But before he could
come, he fell in an ambuscade, a victim to the
treachery of a faithless Lucanian. His slave
soldiers, deeming themselves released from service
by the death of their benefactor, dispersed to their
homes ; his cavalry marched to join the consuls.
Appius and Fulvius, knowing Hannibal to be far
away, advanced boldly into the plain of Capua, but
were driven back to their camp by a bold sally of
the Campanian and Punic horse. In a few days
Hannibal himself appeared on Mount Tifata, and

scattered before him the consular armies, only saved from utter rout by the opportune arrival of Cn. Cornelius with the cavalry of Gracchus's army. He pursued the retreating Appius towards Lucania till that general threw him off and returned to his old position. He then cleared Lucania of Romans by destroying the motley levies of M. Centenius, a promoted centurion, and retired into winter quarters in Apulia. He had gained Capua a respite, but immediately he had gone the Roman eagles gathered round their prey. Reinforced by C. Nero from Suessula, the consuls disposed of 60,000 men, and slowly but surely imprisoned Capua within a double circle of continuous walls. Like the famous lines of the Peloponnesians round Platæa, they resembled a great city enclosing a smaller one within. Late in the winter, when the works were completed, a last offer of pardon was made by the consuls, and refused with scorn by the Capuans. In 211 B.C. Fulvius and Appius Claudius, as pro-consuls, still pressed on the siege, and repulsed the numerous sallies of the Campanian horse.

When spring came, Hannibal himself hastened to succour the beleaguered city. But after a fierce assault on the Roman lines from within and from without had been steadfastly met, the Carthaginians were compelled to draw off by want of provisions.

Hannibal marches ~~me.

Hannibal now resolved to march on Rome. It was perhaps the most daring device of a daring captain. He can hardly have expected to surprise the town, and being without artillery, could gain nothing by a regular siege. But he hoped by this bold movement to draw off the legions from Capua for the defence of the threatened capital. According to Livy, Hannibal crossed the Volturnus in boats, and marched leisurely by the Latin road, spreading havoc far and wide along his track. More probably he moved up the valley of the Volturnus into Samnium, and then crossing the Apennines, swept through the land of the Marsians, passing the ancient city of Alba and the peaceful waters of the Fucine lake. Thence he turned down the valley of the Anio along the Valerian road past Tibur. All accounts agree that he came by the river Anio, crossed the stream, and encamped unmolested within four miles of Rome. Panic reigned in the city: from generation to generation the tale of Hannibal at the gates struck terror to the Roman heart. Yet if Rome trembled, she had still the courage to defy her enemy and to cling with grim tenacity to her half-won prey. Two legions just mustered in the city were ready to repel assault; levies of fugitives (such as the men of Alba Fucens, whom legend has turned into heroes like the Platæans at Marathon) were rapidly raised and armed; order and discipline were speedily restored. From his camp by the Anio, Hannibal rode round the city. He gazed wistfully on the ancient walls which alone saved the houses and temples on the seven hills from destruction, and stood between the people of Rome and his avenging sword. He had driven the iron deep into her soul, and completed her humiliation by wasting her lands and throwing a spear against her gates, but even now he knew he must turn his back on the hated city, and leave his oath of vengeance but half fulfilled. With grateful piety Rome marked the spot on the Appian way where Hannibal drew rein by a shrine to that protecting deity who turned the foe back (Rediculus Tutanus). And as he withdrew from Rome, Hannibal learned that his great manœuvre had not even relieved Capua. Polybius declares that not a man was moved from the besiegers' lines to succour the threatened capital. At any rate the mass of the troops maintained the blockade unbroken, even if it be true that a weak detachment under Fulvius hurried along the Appian way to Rome. Hannibal, as he retired towards Samnium, was cautiously followed by the consul Sulpicius Galba. Frustrated in his last scheme for saving Capua, he turned fiercely on his pursuer, drove him from his camp, and then, by forced marches, hastened to Bruttium in the vain hope of surprising the port of Rhegium.

The Fall of Capua.   The fate of Capua was now sealed. There was now no hope of forcing the Roman lines or of rescue by an army of relief. The fairest city of Italy suffered the last extremity of famine. At

length the starving people surrendered at dis-
cretion to the stern proconsul, Q. Fulvius. The
desertion of the Roman alliance and the murder
of Roman citizens was punished with pitiless
severity. All the leading men of Capua, except
those who had already sought a voluntary death,
died beneath the axe of the executioner, or by
the slower agony of starvation in prison. Their
lands were confiscated, and the people sold as
slaves or deported to distant regions. The plain
became the property of the Roman people; the
city, deprived of its corporate existence and
bereaved of its citizens, was left for the habita-
tion of a mixed multitude of resident aliens
and freedmen, placed under the government of
a præfect annually sent from Rome. Such was
the stern and characteristic decision of the
Senate.

The fall of Capua had a decisive influence on
the course of the war. It terrified the enemies of
Rome, and gave courage to her allies; it tempted
revolted Italians to purchase pardon by a new
treachery, and filled Hannibal with suspicions
even of those who were still true to him. Rome
had recovered her ascendancy over Italy, but the
yet even balance might still be turned, if Hasdrubal, fresh from his Spanish triumphs, should
follow the path of his unconquerable brother, and
join hands with him in a final effort to crush the
power of the enemy

CHAPTER VI

THE WAR FROM THE FALL OF CAPUA TO THE BATTLE OF THE METAURUS

The War in Spain. THE fall of Capua set free a Roman army for service in Spain where help was urgently needed. The reinforcements brought by Mago had driven the legions back on the Ebro (214 B.C.), when a dangerous war with Syphax, a Numidian chieftain, obliged the Carthaginian government to recall Hasdrubal with a part of the Spanish army to Africa (213 B.C.). The Scipios took full advantage of their opportunity : Publius captured Saguntum, while Gnæus spread the dominion of Rome over the tribes of Central Spain. But in 212 B.C. Hasdrubal expelled Syphax from his kingdom, and returned at the head of a victorious army to Spain. In the campaign that followed, the Scipios rashly divided their forces to meet the Punic armies. Deserted by their Spanish mercenaries, the Roman generals were successively attacked and destroyed. A scanty remnant of their armies made good its retreat to the Ebro under a Roman knight, L. Marcius. But the disaster nearly effaced the power of Rome in the peninsula. And even when C. Claudius Nero reached Spain with a legion and 1100 horse, he failed utterly to regain the influence of the Scipios over the Iberian tribes.

Nor were the efforts of Rome crowned with victory in Sicily after the fall of Syracuse. Hannibal, who never lost sight of this important field of war, sent Muttines, a half-caste Liby-Phœnician, to lead the Numidian cavalry serving in the island. The task was brilliantly performed. Marcellus was roughly handled, and the whole land harassed by an unceasing guerrilla warfare. But the foolish pride and jealousy of Hanno, the Carthaginian commander, led to his own defeat in a battle fought on the Himera (211 B.C.) in the absence of Muttines, and to the final loss of Sicily by Carthage. The incapable Carthaginian had dared to deprive Muttines of his command, an affront which the half-caste avenged by betraying Agrigentum (210 B.C.) to the consul Lævinus. Though Hanno and Epicydes escaped to Carthage, their soldiers were surprised and slaughtered, and Lævinus surpassed at Agrigentum the cruelties wrought by Marcellus at Syracuse. The blow was decisive. Sicily was tranquillised, it became an oppressed but submissive province. Confiscation and robbery, speculation and slave-farming, sowed seed that later was destined to bear bitter fruit in the horrible atrocities of the Servile wars.

In 210 B.C., Rome, exhausted by the long struggle and distracted by the many calls upon her forces abroad, placed but four legions in the field against Hannibal. Marcellus, who received a well-deserved ovation for the capture of Syra-

cuse, regained Salapia by treachery, and took
some small fortresses in Samnium. But Hannibal, with admirable judgment, drew in his troops
from his more distant garrisons, and by this timely
concentration again made himself supreme in the
field. Advancing rapidly against the pro-consul
Cn. Fulvius Centumalus, he surprised him near
Herdonea,* and by a brilliant flank attack routed
the army, slew the general, and captured the camp
of the enemy. Too late to save his colleague,
Marcellus hastened to Lucania in the hope of
retrieving the disaster. In a fierce combat on
the Numistro, he upheld the honour of the Roman
arms, but suffered heavy losses, and with diminished strength was compelled to leave Hannibal
master of the open country.

Distress
and Dis-
content in
Italy.

The drain of unceasing war was gradually exhausting the resources of Rome and undermining
the loyalty of her truest allies. In 210 B.C. the
people doggedly refused to pay the 'ship money'
imposed, and the necessary funds for manning
and fitting out a fleet had to be raised by the
free-will offerings of patriotic citizens, headed by
the consul Lævinus. Next year the government
appropriated the reserve fund (4000 lbs. of gold)
laid by in better times to meet the last necessities
of the State. The worst was yet to come. When
the consuls called on the Latins to furnish troops

* The earlier defeat of another Fulvius at Herdonea (212 B.C.) is
probably this battle erroneously dated.

and supplies for the coming campaign, the deputies of twelve cities bluntly answered that they had neither men nor money left. The refusal threatened the existence of Rome and the maintenance of Latin supremacy in Italy. Whatever were the causes of Latin discontent, it plainly prevailed chiefly among the older and nearer colonies in Latium, Northern Campania, Etruria and the Marsic land. The fate of Rome hung upon the answer made by the eighteen remaining Latin cities to the anxious question of the consuls. In their name, Sextilius of Fregellæ declared that men and money were forthcoming, and that they had means enough, and will more than enough, to fulfil every order and wish of the Roman people. With noble and far-sighted patriotism, the Latin colonists in distant Gaul and Picenum, and the great fortresses of Southern Italy, remained true to the cause of the Italian nation and Latin leadership. While with severe moderation the recalcitrant cities were left alone to repent at leisure of their want of zeal, the faithful colonies received the solemn thanks of the Roman Senate and people. Rome, assured of their fidelity, could face with equanimity the growing agitation in Etruria; and when the conspiracy came to a head at Arretium, the town was garrisoned, the country held down, and the attempted revolution nipped in the bud (208 B.C.).

For the campaign of 209 B.C., Rome placed her
most trusted generals, Fabius, Fulvius and Marcellus, at the head of three full consular armies.
Marcellus was to confront Hannibal in Apulia,
while Fulvius reduced Lucania and Fabius besieged
Tarentum. Hannibal was greatly outnumbered,
but he did not tamely allow himself to be cooped
up in Apulia and gradually deprived of the bases
of his operations. He saw that his enemies were
divided, and might be attacked and beaten in
detail. So he fell fiercely on Marcellus, and in
two well fought engagements so disabled him that
he lay helpless at Venusia for the rest of the summer. After thus ridding himself of one enemy,
Hannibal hurried into Bruttium to relieve Caulonia.
The motley levies sent from Sicily by Lævinus
abandoned the siege at the mere news of his
approach, but flight did not save them from pursuit
and capture. Hannibal then marched back with
all haste to Tarentum, rather in the hope of crush-
ing Fabius before its walls than from fear lest so
strong a place should fall into the enemy's hands.
When he was within five miles of the town, he
was bitterly undeceived. A Bruttian captain had
treacherously sold Tarentum to the Romans, and
Carthalo, the Punic commandant, with Nicon and
Philemenus, who had opened the gates to Hannibal,
fell in the general massacre which followed the
capture of the town. The news of the loss of the
city which secured his communications with Carth-

age and Macedon was as heavy a blow to Hannibal as the surrender of Paris was to Napoleon as he hastened to its relief. Yet, not suffering himself to be misled by fear or passion, Hannibal endeavoured to lure Fabius into an ambush by a pretended offer from Metapontum to betray the town and Punic garrison. The wary veteran all but fell into the snare, but discovered at the last moment that the omens were adverse. He was content with the success he had won, with the booty of 3000 talents and the 30,000 slaves taken at Tarentum. Henceforth he retired from service in the field, though retaining great weight in the councils of the Roman State.

Disappointment at the failure of the Roman generals to beat Hannibal in battle found vent Death of Marcellus. in a bill to depose Marcellus, but the people, full of sympathy for the brave old warrior who never shrank from attacking his invincible opponent, not only threw out the bill, but elected Marcellus consul along with T. Quinctius Crispinus. The object of the campaign was the capture of Locri in Bruttium, the chief seaport now left in Hannibal's possession. Yet Crispinus, who began the siege, was forced by the approach of the Carthaginians to retire and join his colleague near Venusia. Again, when the legion at Tarentum marched thence to co-operate with the Sicilian fleet in the siege of Locri, Hannibal boldly detached from his main body in front of Venusia 3000 foot and 2000 horse, who by a well-laid ambush near Petelia utterly destroyed or dispersed the ill-fated legion. The two main armies lay near Venusia, divided by a wooded hill. The consuls, anxious to secure this position, rode forward with a small escort to reconnoitre the ground beyond from the crest. Meanwhile, screened by the trees, a body of Numidians stole round the hill and fell suddenly on the rear of the astonished enemy. Marcellus was killed on the spot, Crispinus rode off only to die of his wounds in camp. The Roman armies retired dispirited, while Hannibal flew once more to relieve Locri, and forced the besiegers to abandon their works and take refuge in their ships. Rome had lost the bravest of her soldiers —the man who in her darkest hour had never despaired of her safety, nor flinched from the conflict with her victorious enemy. Marcellus has been charged with treachery with cruelty and with greed, the common vices of his age and country; but much may be forgiven to the strong hand which slew the Gallic chief and dedicated the spoils to Jupiter Feretrius, and to the intrepid spirit which, sleeping 'or waking, had but one thought, one hope—the defeat of Hannibal and the salvation of Rome. His great antagonist ordered the body of Marcellus to be honourably burned and the ashes sent to his son.

Character of Scipio. While fortune thus shifted to and fro in Italy, great events were happening in Spain. Rome needed a leader of no common gifts to counteract the skilled diplomacy and military ability of Hasdrubal Barca. The tide of war had rolled back from the Tagus to the Ebro ; might not yet greater danger be threatened by the determined efforts made at Carthage to raise recruits for Hasdrubal ? The Senate resolved to leave to the assembly the choice of an officer to fill this difficult and important post, and the choice fell on young P. Scipio. We may disregard the story that he only offered himself as a candidate because none other could be found to undertake the task. Rome was not so poor in tried soldiers and statesmen, nor was patriotism so dead, that they should shrink from the post of danger and of glory. In truth the popularity of his dead kinsmen in Spain, and the influence of the great Cornelian house in Rome, pointed unmistakably to the employment of the daring and distinguished young officer. Yet his want of rank and standing made it necessary to constrain the people by an apparently free and unpremeditated choice to advance the mere military tribune and ex-ædile to the most independent and responsible pro-consular command. Never was the choice of Senate and people more fully justified by the event. Scipio was not indeed one of those creative spirits who mould for centuries the destinies of mankind, nor even one of those who profoundly affect their own age and country. Though brilliantly successful as a soldier, in genius for war he was infinitely inferior to Hannibal, whom it was his destiny to conquer. In politics, he had not the far-seeing eye or the master-mind of a Cæsar or an Alexander, nor yet the self-restraint and moderation to accept the restrictions imposed by a republican constitution. Nevertheless, a dazzling halo of serene and assured inspiration encircles the head of the young hero. As a diplomatist, he rivalled Marlborough in skill and refinement. As a ruler, he drew the half-tamed races of Spain into allegiance to Rome by kindly sympathy and wise generosity. As a man he was steadfast to his word, and royal in his bearing. Confident of his divine mission, he allowed his simpler fellow-countrymen to believe him the special favourite of the gods, endowed by them with supernatural foresight. His solitary and kingly spirit dwelt apart from and above the crowd, but his charm and grace of manner, however un-Roman, won the hearts of his own countrymen as well as of foreigners. His many gifts, and not least the gift of invariable good fortune, made him the victor in this momentous war and the saviour of his country. The heaven-sent hero set sail for Spain in 211-10 B.C. at the head of 11,000 men and 30 ships of war, taking with him the pro-prætor M. Silanus as adjutant and adviser, and C. Lælius to command his fleet.

Capture of New Carthage. Scipio at once justified his selection by a brilliant and daring feat. While he was wintering at Tarraco, he learned that the Punic armies were stationed far apart, and far from their military base and the key of their communications, New Carthage. Mago was near the pillars of Hercules, Hasdrubal Gisgo at the mouth of the Tagus, and Hasdrubal Barca not far from its source, at least ten days' march from the capital. Here were their dockyards and arsenals, their treasures and magazines, with 300 Spanish hostages, all committed to the protection of an insignificant garrison. At the dawn of spring (210 B.C.), before the Punic armies were stirring, Scipio secretly crossed the Ebro at the head of 27,500 men, supported by a fleet of 35 sail. So swift was his march that he reached New Carthage before the Punic generals had news of his advance. The town of Cartagena stands at the head of a famous harbour, built partly on five hills of moderate height, and partly on the low ground beneath them. To the north there is now a large extent of alluvial land (the Almajar) drained by a canal, but in the days of Scipio this was a shallow lagoon, whose waters sank at the ebb, since it communicated with the port. Thus the town lay on a peninsula, washed by the sea on the south and west, and joined to the mainland by a narrow isthmus. Scipio encamped at the head of this isthmus, and beat back a desperate sally of the garrison, but failed in his first assault on the high walls of the town. But in the afternoon, under cover of a renewed assault by land and sea, Scipio sent 500 men to cross the lagoon at low water, and scale the undefended walls. These men opened the main gate to their comrades outside, and the town was won; whereupon the governor surrendered the citadel.

Clemency of Scipio. Ere nightfall Scipio checked massacre and plunder. The Romans gained possession of a fleet, abundant stores of corn, a large sum of money, and many engines of war. To the 10,000 captives Scipio showed unexampled clemency; only the Carthaginian officers and soldiers were sent as prisoners to Rome; the craftsmen were ordered to re-arm the legionaries with the Spanish sword and to equip an increased number of men and ships; the seafaring population were pressed to man the fleet; but all were promised eventually the liberty accorded at once to the citizens of New Carthage. The Spanish hostages were treated with delicate courtesy, and assured of a safe return to their homes, so soon as their countrymen should embrace the Roman alliance. The young hero conquered the hearts of the impulsive Iberians by kindness more effectually than by the sword. For the rest of the year Scipio lay quiet, strengthening his influence over the Spanish chiefs. The Punic generals were paralysed by his capture of New Carthage (which forced them to draw their supplies from distant Gades) and debarred from effective co-operation by mutual jealousy.

Encouraged by the success of the previous year, Scipio in 209 B.C. resolved to forsake the wise and cautious policy of defending the line of the Ebro, and hazard all by taking the offensive. He laid up his fleet that he might draft his best seamen into the legions, and after being joined on the march by two powerful Spanish chieftains, Mandonius and Indibilis, moved southwards in search of Hasdrubal. He found him strongly posted at Bæcula on the Upper Guadalquiver. In the engagement that followed, Scipio claimed the victory, but whatever was the result of the actual fighting, he was clearly outmanœuvred and out-generalled. Hasdrubal, with his war-chest his elephants and his best troops, made his way northward over the Tagus, and thence marched unpursued and unobserved by the western passes of the Pyrenees near San Sebastian to winter quietly in Gaul. Scipio, who must have known that Hasdrubal's great object was to join his brother in Italy, should have brought him to bay at all costs, or, if that was impossible, he should have hung upon his rear and dogged his footsteps. But either from weakness or ignorance he contented himself with closing the eastern passes of the Pyrenees and the line of the Segre, leaving the western route open to the Carthaginian. By this unpardonable blunder Scipio exposed Italy to a combined attack by the two sons of Hamilcar, and endangered the very existence of Rome. Yet

Fortune crowned even the errors of her favourite with laurels. The departure of Hasdrubal Barca made it easy for Scipio to conquer Spain; the peril of his presence in Italy was averted by Nero on the banks of the Metaurus.

Rome pre-
pares to
meet Has-
drubal.

The next year Hasdrubal spent among the Arverni, busily raising soldiers. Warned of the fact by their faithful allies, the men of Massilia, the Senate prepared to face the last and greatest crisis of the war, and to measure swords with both the sons of Hamilcar in Italy. Men's hearts were faint for fear, the land lay waste, the supply of recruits began to fail, yet Rome faltered not, but put forth all her strength in one supreme effort. By drawing 11,000 men from Spain and 4000 from Sicily, by the enrolment of slaves, by the enforcement of the levy even in the maritime colonies usually exempt, fifteen legions were gathered to meet the foe in Italy, while eight more were serving aboard. Nor was there greater difficulty in raising forces than in finding generals fit to command the last armies of the Republic. Rome had lost her sword and shield for Marcellus was dead and Fabius enfeebled by age. The choice of the people fell on C. Claudius Nero, who had seen service before Capua and in Spain, and on a stern and sullen old man, M. Livius Salinator, whose triumph over the Illyrians had been followed by an unjust condemnation for embezzlement of the spoil. Still nursing his sense of wrong, Livius was with difficulty drawn from his retirement and reconciled to his colleague. The lot decided that Livius should face Hasdrubal and Nero Hannibal. The Roman generals had the advantage of larger numbers, better troops and interior lines. Nero confronted Hannibal with four double legions, while two more threatened the Carthaginian rear; Livius and Porcius, with four legions, were to check Hasdrubal's advance, while Varro held down Etruria and menaced his flank; two legions lay in reserve at Rome and one at Capua. It was obviously most difficult, even for such great masters in the art of war as the two brothers, to unite their divided armies. An opportunity was offered to the Romans, such as Napoleon ever sought, of holding one enemy in check with a part of their force, while the other was crushed by the concentration of superior numbers marching on inner lines.

Hasdrubal left his winter quarters in Gaul early, Advance and crossed the Alps with surprising ease and of Has-drubal. speed. The mountaineers had now learned that the strangers merely passed through their valleys on their way to assail distant enemies, and meant them no harm. But when he had reached the valley of the Po, Hasdrubal lost time in the siege of Placentia. He may have hoped by its reduction to win the unanimous support of the Celts; he may have feared to leave behind him a strong fortress which might menace his retreat; he was

undoubtedly gathering to his standards Gauls and
Ligurians.   Nevertheless, the waste of time involved in the siege, and the discredit incurred by
his failure to take the town, seriously affected the
subsequent course of the campaign.   At length
Hasdrubal advanced towards Ariminum at the
head of some 50,000 men, but he was weak in
cavalry and elephants, and his infantry was largely
composed of undisciplined and unstable Gauls.
The prætor, L. Porcius, fell back before his
advance until he reached the camp of the consul
Livius, near Sena Gallica.   Hasdrubal had sent
some horsemen to tell his brother of his approach,
and to propose that they should join hands in
Umbria, and march by Narnia on Rome.

Move-
ments of
Hannibal.

In South Italy, Hannibal, in face of Nero's
superior force, moved hither and thither through
Lucania and Bruttium, gathering together his
scattered garrisons and allies.   Nero attempted to
check his advance by attacking him at Grumentum
on the Aciris, but, in spite of a reported victory,
was clearly beaten off and eluded.   Hannibal,
closely followed by the consul, advanced as far as
Canusium in Apulia.   While he had no definite
information, he dare not leave his allies and strongholds in the south defenceless: he waited to hear
by what route his brother was coming, in order
that they might act together, and by concerted
movements overwhelm the Roman armies.

March of

But Hasdrubal's bold troopers, after safely

traversing the length of Italy, were captured near
Tarentum. The despatches found upon them
containing Hasdrubal's plan of operations were
forwarded and read to the consul. Whether the
movements of the armies in the north were
already known to Nero or not, the capture of
these messengers, which proved Hannibal's ignorance and secured its continuance, was of supreme
importance. And in this crisis of his country's
fate Nero showed himself a great captain. He
might have waited for orders from the Senate,
he might have sent reinforcements to his colleague
and remained himself to face Hannibal, but he
at once resolved to take the flower of his army
and help Livius to crush Hasdrubal. He urged
the Senate to recall the legion of Capua to Rome,
and send the city legions to hold Narnia against
the invaders. He then picked out 6000 footmen and 1000 horse for a pretended raid
into Lucania, and hastened by forced marches
northwards, while he left the bulk of his army to
resist Hannibal. Life and death hung upon his
speed, and every effort was made to ensure success.
The soldiers, when told by the consul whither they
were going, felt all the glory of their mission, and
marched day and night, scarcely staying for food
or rest. The whole population crowded to the
roadside and welcomed them as deliverers, pressing
on them meat and drink, horses and carriages.
Veterans and youths flocked to the colours. After

a week's march Nero reached his colleague's camp
and entered it under cover of night, thus conceal-
ing his coming from Hasdrubal as skilfully as he
had hidden his departure from Hannibal.   At
the council of war Livius wished to give the
weary troops a rest, but Nero, in fear lest Hannibal should follow him, insisted on immediate
battle.

Hasdrubal
retreats to
the Me-
taurus.

The two armies were now drawn up in front of
their camps, with but half a mile ¡between them.
But when Hasdrubal rode forward to reconnoitre,
his soldier's eye marked the increased numbers of
the Romans, and the travel-stained arms and tired
horses of Nero's cavalry.   His suspicions were
confirmed by the twice-sounded trumpet in the
camp of Livius, which satisfied him that both
consuls were before him.   Unable to believe that
Nero had eluded Hannibal, Hasdrubal resolved
to retreat to the Metaurus.   He might yet hear
that Hannibal was in full march to join him, in
which case a flank movement along the Flaminian
road would enable him to turn the Roman position and meet his brother in Umbria.   Or, if the
worst had happened and Hannibal had fallen,
Hasdrubal might either accept battle behind the
Metaurus, or retreat into Cisalpine Gaul.   At
nightfall he decamped, resolved to steal a march
on the enemy.   But in the confusion his guides
escaped, and when he reached the Metaurus no
ford could be found, either by reason of the dark-

ness or because the river was in flood. The bed of the Metaurus is like a trough, sunk between steep cliffs, far below the general surface of the valley through which the river winds. Two thousand years ago the stream did not loiter quietly through a cultivated plain, but ran swift and strong through thick uncleared forests. Hasdrubal's columns slowly wound along the wooded cliffs, till, hopeless of crossing, he encamped in a strong position on the right bank, perhaps at Monte St Angelo.

Here Hasdrubal was overtaken by the Roman cavalry, closely followed by the legions. He made the best of a dangerous situation. His Gallic infantry, whose ranks had been thinned on the night march by desertion and drunkenness, he stationed on his left in a position too strong to be assailed in front, and covered in flank by the river. The Ligurians and elephants formed the centre, the right wing, composed of Spanish and African veterans, was drawn up on lower and more open ground. Hasdrubal formed his troops in deep files with narrow front, and attacked Livius and Porcius with desperate courage. Long and obstinate was the struggle between the legions and the Spaniards, while the elephants, galled by missiles, trampled down friend and foe alike. At length Nero, after a vain attempt to storm the hill which protected the Gauls, drew off his picked troops, and, passing round behind the Roman

Battle of the Metaurus.

line, flung them with decisive effect on Hasdrubal's flank and rear.

The Spaniards, outnumbered and surrounded, were cut to pieces, resisting to the last ; the drunken Gauls were slaughtered helpless and inert. Seeing the day was lost, Hasdrubal spurred his horse into the Roman ranks and met a soldier's death, as became a son of Hamilcar and a brother of Hannibal.

Hannibal learns of his Brother's Death. With no less haste than he had come, Nero returned to confront Hannibal in Apulia. He sullied the glory of the great victory, due to his daring and original strategy, by a cruel and ignoble deed. The head of Hasdrubal was flung to the Punic outposts, a truly Claudian return for Hannibal's generous treatment of Marcellus's corpse. When Hannibal beheld the ghastly relic, he recognised the coming doom of his house and of his country. His lofty schemes of conquest crumbled to the dust, the age-long struggle of Aryan and Semite was for the time decided. But Hannibal had no time for idle tears. He speedily evacuated Apulia and Lucania, and drew together every available man to his last refuge in Italy, the land of the Bruttii.

Triumph at Rome. At Rome the anxiety had been poignant when men heard of Nero's march, nor was the agony of suspense ended by the first vague rumours of victory. But when despatches came from the consuls to announce that the Punic army had

been destroyed and the general killed, the Roman
people dared to breathe again, and in the exultation of the moment almost forgot that Hannibal
was still in Italy. At the end of the year the
consuls celebrated the first real triumph of the war.
Once more the long array of shouting soldiers
followed their generals through the streets up to
the temple of Capitoline Jove, while spoils trophies
and captives were borne before them. Livius
drove in the royal chariot with the four white
steeds, since the victory was won in his province,
but the multitude saluted as the true conqueror
the colleague who rode on horseback at his side.
Nevertheless Nero, whose genius for war eclipsed
all other Romans hitherto opposed to Hannibal,
was never again given a command. The star of
Scipio was in the ascendant, that of the victor on
the Metaurus paled before it.

CHAPTER VII

THE CLOSE OF THE HANNIBALIC WAR

Scipio in Spain.

IN 208 B.C., little occurred in Spain. Hasdrubal Barca had crossed the Pyrenees, Mago withdrew to the Baliaric Isles, and Hasdrubal Gisgo to Lusitania; only Massinissa and his Numidian horse carried on a desultory warfare. Thus Scipio, though weakened by the despatch of reinforcements to Italy, remained master of the eastern coast. At Tarraco he held an almost royal court, and by his lofty courtesy and consciousness of greatness gained the enthusiastic admiration of the chivalrous Spaniards. In 207 B.C., Hanno brought over from Africa a third army, and with Mago's help attempted to stir up the Celtiberian tribes. But M. Silanus surprised and captured Hanno, and dispersed his levies, whereupon Hasdrubal Gisgo, afraid to risk a battle, broke up his force into detachments, with which he garrisoned the towns of Andalusia. L. Scipio closed the campaign with credit by storming the strongest of these fortresses, Oringis.

Victory of Scipio.

In the following year, 206 B.C., P. Scipio, by an ingenious and elaborate tactical manœuvre, gained a great and crowning victory. By vigorous efforts the Punic generals had gathered together some 70,000 troops, while the Romans had but 50,000. Both forces contained a large number of Spanish levies. They met on the Upper Bætis, at a place probably called Ilipa or Silpia. For several days the armies confronted one another with their Spanish recruits on the wings, and their best troops, Roman or African, massed in the centre. But Scipio had determined, like Wellington, to use the Spaniards merely to impose on the enemy, and to strike the decisive blow with his veterans. Accordingly, under cover of darkness he placed his Spaniards in the centre and his legions on the wings. Remembering the lesson of the Trebia, he had given his soldiers a good meal, when at daybreak he pushed forward his cavalry and light troops to draw the enemy from their camp. Without staying to eat, the Carthaginians hastily poured forth from their tents and formed in their usual order of battle. As Scipio moved against them, he withdrew his screen of skirmishers and reformed his cavalry and light troops behind his legions. Suddenly the legions on the right and left advanced *en échelon*, with the cavalry guarding their flanks, while the Spaniards in the centre held back. Thus, while the centre stood motionless and inactive, Scipio's Romans in oblique line charged the unsteady Spaniards on the enemy's wings and broke them utterly. In their flight they swept away the Africans in the centre, and the Punic

army ceased to exist. The leaders fled to Gades,
the Spaniards deserted a cause now obviously
lost, and Scipio reported to the Senate that the
war in Spain was over.

Scipio now turned his eyes to Africa. He
sent Lælius to make overtures to Syphax, the
Numidian prince whose earlier hostility to Carthage had been severely punished. Hearing that
Syphax would only treat with the Roman general
in person, Scipio himself crossed to Africa after a
narrow escape from a Carthaginian squadron. At
the table of Syphax the Roman met Hasdrubal
Gisgo bent on the same errand. The charms of
Hasdrubal's daughter Sophonisba weighed more
with the amorous Numidian than Scipio's elo-
quence, and Syphax become the firm friend of
Carthage. Scipio's failure was to some extent
redeemed by the adhesion of the rival Numidian
chieftain Massinissa.

Within the same year Mago succeeded in reviving the dying embers of the war in Andalusia.
Scipio found himself obliged to reduce Illiturgi,
Castulo and Astapa. Graver dangers than the
desperate resistance of isolated towns soon
threatened the peace of Spain. Late in the
summer Scipio fell ill, and at the news a division
of Italian troops quartered near the Sucro mutinied
on the pretext that their pay was in arrears, and
chose two common soldiers as their generals.
Scipio invited the mutineers to New Carthage

to receive their arrears of pay, quietly surrounded them with loyal soldiers, and finally quelled the mutiny by the execution of thirty-five ringleaders and the grant of a free pardon to the repentant soldiery. He at once led his men against the Spanish chieftains then in arms, Mandonius and Indibilis, whose fidelity to Rome had rested on their attachment to his person, and by a bloody victory compelled them to sue for mercy.

When Mago saw that nothing came of these revolts, he despaired of holding Gades against the Romans. By order of the home government he gathered together every man and every shekel he could raise, and set sail for Italy, bent on a last vain effort to join hands with Hannibal. Scipio now paid the penalty for dismantling his fleet, in seeing another son of Hamilcar depart unopposed to invade Italy. Mago, after a futile attempt to surprise New Carthage, wintered in the Baliaric Isles, and next spring landed at Genoa to stir up revolt in Liguria and Cisalpine Gaul. After his departure, Gades made terms with the new masters of Spain, and the realm won by the Barcid house for Carthage passed into the hands of their enemies. Scipio returned to Rome, and though through senatorial pedantry denied a formal triumph because he had not held the qualifying magistracy, the young conqueror was welcomed with acclamations by the people, and at once elected consul for the ensuing year, 205 B.C.

Spain finally subdued.

The final loss of Spain—a great blow to Carthage
—was soon followed by the desertion of Macedon.
The Ætolians and other Greek allies of Rome, weary
of a war at once cruel, objectless and burdensome,
patched up a peace with Philip, who took the opportunity to come to terms with Rome. The king
gained some worthless territory at the cost of the
betrayal of his great ally, and the opening of the
Greek world to Roman ambition.

Hannibal
in Brut-
tium.
In one quarter of the Mediterranean world only
was Rome still successfully defied, and that in
Italy itself by Hannibal. Had the Senate flung
the united and victorious armies of Livius and
Nero upon him at once, he could scarcely have
escaped destruction. But after the long strain,
moral and material, on the energies of the people,
a reaction set in. Diminished armies lay inactive
in front of Hannibal. The Roman government
applied itself to the revival of agriculture, the
reorganisation of the finances and the repayment
of loans. The long-delayed punishment at length
fell on the Roman citizens who had defrauded
the State, and on the twelve Latin towns whose
fidelity had wavered at the crisis of the war. For
four long years Hannibal maintained his hold on
Bruttium. Never was his superiority to fortune
more manifest, never was his control over men
more marvellous. His name still inspired confidence and affection in his motley levies, and still
struck with terror the overwhelming forces of the

enemy. He evacuated Thurii, he lost Locri through treachery and the boldness of Scipio. But as Wellington in the lines of Torres Vedras bade defiance to the French, so Hannibal, entrenched in his camp near the Lacinian promontory, still set a limit to the power of Rome. Without assistance from false allies or from his own feeble countrymen, sustained by a noble pride and faith in his own genius, he clung with desperate tenacity to his last foothold on Italian soil.

At Rome (205 B.C.) Scipio entered office with the firm resolve to carry out the invasion of Africa which he had planned in Spain. But the consul met with a determined opposition in the Senate. Romans of the old school despised his modern culture, and suspected him of demagogic arts. They disliked his arbitrary conduct of the war in Spain, and condemned with bitterness the laxity of his discipline. No doubt there was some justice in the contention of Fabius that Hannibal should first be expelled from Italy, nevertheless the quickest way to attain this end was to attack Carthage where she was most vulnerable in Africa. But if Rome meditated a blow at the heart of Carthage, she should have struck with her full force. Otherwise she exposed her army of invasion to the chance of a disaster like that of Regulus. Hannibal might bring his veterans from Italy, and Syphax might launch swarms of Numidian horsemen to overwhelm the bold in-

Scipio plans the Invasion of Africa.

vader on the bare plains of Libya. Nevertheless the Senate had not the magnanimity to forgive the ambitious consul for threatening to appeal to the people against its decision, nor the wisdom to see that in such a case it must trust all or nothing. It took refuge in a weak compromise, and permitted the expedition which it neither sanctioned nor organised. The consul was given timber for a fleet from the State forests, and furnished with stores and arms by the suspected cities in Etruria, which eagerly vindicated their character for patriotism by an anxious liberality. By these means Scipio created a new fleet of thirty sail. From his province of Sicily he was allowed to take two legions, which he strengthened by drafts from the survivors of Cannæ, and 7000 veterans who volunteered for the service. Scipio spent a year in drilling and organising this inadequate force, regarded by his enemies in the Senate as a forlorn hope, whose destruction would be no great loss to the State.

The fear of invasion inspired the Punic government with a feverish energy. To secure Numidia, Syphax was drawn more closely to Carthage, and Massinissa driven from his kingdom to become a homeless wanderer in the desert. Besides a Numidian contingent, a Macedonian corps under Sopater and some Celtiberian mercenaries were expected to reinforce the home army.

Mago in
Italy.

Meanwhile in Italy, Mago, who had landed at

Genoa with 14,000 men, was rapidly drawing Gauls and Ligurians to his standards. The youngest of the lion-brood of Hamilcar strove even at the eleventh hour to fulfil the vengeance vowed by his father. But Lævinus and Livius with six legions held the old defensive positions at Ariminum and Arretium, and Mago was too weak to attack them. In vain he tampered with Etruscan malcontents, and tempted the Gauls to action by working on their love of gold and of adventure. When the final message of recall reached him, a bloody defeat in the land of the Insubres had forced on him a long and difficult retreat to Genoa. In the lost battle Mago himself was struck down, and died of his wounds on the homeward voyage.

Nor again was Hannibal able to divert Scipio from his purpose. At Locri the two great captains first crossed swords. The citizens had betrayed the town and one of its citadels to Scipio, while the Punic garrison still held a second citadel. When Hannibal attempted to recover the town by a concerted attack from within and from without, he was driven off with some loss by Scipio, who sallied out and took the scaling party in rear. Nevertheless, the exploit nearly ended in the disgrace of the victor. Plunder and outrage were openly encouraged by Scipio's lieutenant, Q. Pleminius, and passed unpunished by the general. The looseness of

Capture of Locri.

Scipio's discipline and even his personal character were fiercely attacked in the Senate by Fabius. But the commission of inquiry threw all the blame on Pleminius, and far from recalling Scipio to stand his trial, gave a glowing account of his work in preparing for the invasion of Africa.

Scipio lands in Africa.

At last, in 204 B.C., Scipio set sail from Lilybæum with 40 warships, 400 transports, and an army of some 35,000 men. He landed without encountering the faintest opposition, and after a successful cavalry combat, laid siege to the ancient town of Utica. But the difficulties of the campaign had been under-valued, and the force at Scipio's disposal was too small to maintain the siege, and at the same time assume the offensive. The Phœnicians had proved more than once that they could fight with dogged obstinacy in defence of hearth and home. On this occasion, the stubborn resistance of Utica gave Syphax and Hasdrubal time to mass together large, if ill-disciplined, forces for the relief of the town. Scipio found himself obliged to retire for the winter to a headland between Utica and Carthage, and entrench himself there in a position known as the Cornelian camp. He was 'hemmed in if not surrounded,' dependent for his supplies on the command of the sea, and the support of a lukewarm government at home. Had Hannibal learned his real position, he might have returned from Italy to crush the presumptuous invader of Africa.

Massinissa, who had joined the Romans with a small band of horsemen, now proved his value. Scipio, availing himself of the knowledge and arts of the wily barbarian, resolved to play upon the weakness of his opponents. He stilled the fears of the Carthaginians with proposals for peace, and flattered the vanity of Syphax by making him the mediator of the pretended treaty. But the terms proposed, the reciprocal evacuation of Italy and Africa, could not have been entertained by the Roman government, or seriously intended by Scipio. The negotiations served a darker purpose. While envoys passed to and fro, Roman spies observed and reported the position and arrangement of the hostile armies. At length, when he had lulled Syphax and Hasdrubal to a fatal security, Scipio broke off the negotiations, and planned a night attack on their camps. The wooden huts thatched with reeds suddenly burst into flames, and as the unhappy Africans fled from the fire, they were slaughtered by the Roman divisions, which had stealthily surrounded them. Massinissa was the soul of an enterprise which has cast a slur on the good faith of Scipio. Yet, however dishonourable the stratagem, its success was indubitable. The armies of Syphax and Hasdrubal could not have kept the field had it not been for the opportune arrival of their Macedonian and Celtiberian auxiliaries. Thus reinforced, they ventured to offer battle, but were scattered to the winds by Scipio on the 'Great Plains' (203 B.C.). Syphax, fleeing to seek shelter among his tribesmen, was closely pursued and captured by Lælius and Massinissa. The beauteous Sophonisba was the prize of victory, but the last and only service Massinissa could do his old love and newly wedded bride was to save her from gracing a Roman triumph by sending her poison. Massinissa was restored to his throne by the Romans, and proved his gratitude by raising some thousands of admirable light horsemen to serve beneath their banners.

Negotiations for Peace.

Meanwhile, Scipio occupied Tunis, and with some difficulty repulsed an attack on his fleet near Utica, by lashing his transport ships together in a line four deep, and manning this boom with troops. But both sides were now eager to treat. At Carthage the peace party, long silenced, again made itself heard, and on the other side Scipio was anxious to have the credit of ending the war. Whether influenced by this selfish motive or by a generous and wise moderation, the Roman general offered most favourable terms. Carthage was to cede Spain and the islands of the Western Mediterranean, to recognise Massinissa as lord of the whole realm of Numidia, to surrender her fleet except twenty vessels, and to pay a war indemnity of 4000 talents. She would retain her trade her wealth and her African empire. We cannot wonder that there was strong opposition in the Senate to conditions so lenient. Yet weariness of war and the commanding influence of Scipio would seem to have procured their approval , by the people, and even to have wrung a reluctant consent from the Senate.

But it was now too late. During these prolonged debates the war party at Carthage had rallied, and had resolved to risk all on a last despairing throw. The sons of Hamilcar were recalled from Italy to meet the· Romans in Africa. Mago did not live to reach his native land, but his troops returned to fight under his brother in his last great battle. Hannibal himself obeyed without delay the order of recall. His latest hopes of overthrowing the Roman power in Italy had vanished with the defection of Philip and the defeat of Mago. He must now return to save, if it were still possible, his ill-fated country from the consequences of her errors and her weakness. In the temple of Juno, on the Lacinian Cape, he left a record of his exploits engraved on tables of bronze, still to be seen in the days of Polybius. With a heavy heart he turned his back on the scene of his triumphs, to face an agony worse than death. The country which, in spite of her faults and failures, he loved to the last, was about to bow her neck beneath the yoke of that unconquerable people whose

Recall of Hannibal.

spirit rose ever higher after defeat, and by its constancy overcame the genius of its greatest foe. Hannibal sailed from Croton, taking with him some 25,000 men. It is but an idle slander that he massacred those Italians who refused to follow him over sea, though it is possible they preferred death by their own hands to the tender mercies of Rome. Freed from the terror of his presence, the Senate and people bestowed on the veteran Fabius a wreath of grass, a last tribute of gratitude to the saviour of his country. Within the year Fabius died (203 B.C.).

Rupture of the Negotiations Hannibal landed in the bay of Leptis and concentrated his forces at Hadrumetum. To strengthen his cavalry he entered into relations with Vermina, the son of Syphax, and other sheiks of the desert, and thus obtained some 2000 Numidian horse, with the promise of further aid. But he needed time to weld together Mago's mercenaries the Carthaginian militia and his own Italians. In the spring (202 B.C.) the hungry mob of Carthage plundered a shipwrecked Roman convoy. Anxious to avoid a rupture, Scipio merely demanded satisfaction for this breach of the armistice. But the Carthaginian government made war inevitable by the refusal of his reasonable request, and by a treacherous attack on the ship which bore back his envoys. Scipio at once resumed operations, and marched to meet Massinissa, spreading terror and desolation along

the valley of the Bagradas. Hannibal, who rejoiced to see the Roman army severed from its
maritime base, pressed forward towards Zama
to prevent the junction of the two hostile armies,
and to pick up his own Numidian horse. He
found the allies had already united, and encamped
near Naraggara. The great Carthaginian sought
an interview with his youthful rival. At this
memorable conference he offered, on behalf of
Carthage, to resign all possessions outside Africa.
Scipio, though fully aware that defeat on the
open plain far from the sea meant destruction,
resolutely refused to allow Carthage to profit by
her breach of the truce. Honour and policy
alike impelled Rome to demand satisfaction for
the past, and guarantees for the future.

The decisive struggle took place in the summer
of 202 B.C., on the plains of Zama, near Sicca.
The strength of the two armies was not unequal,
for if Hannibal was superior in numbers, he was
weak in cavalry, and some of his troops were untrustworthy. He had in all some 50,000 men,
of whom 5000 were horsemen, with 80 elephants.
Scipio commanded 30,000 legionaries, 10,000
horsemen and perhaps 5000 light-armed auxiliaries. Hannibal's dispositions were admirably
adapted to the circumstances. He formed his
infantry in three solid lines. In the van stood
Mago's mercenaries, 12,000 strong; in support
was the Libyan and Punic militia, with the

The
Armies at
Zama.

Macedonian contingent; in reserve, some distance
behind, were posted the 20,000 veterans who had
followed Hannibal from Italy.   The front was
covered by the formidable line of elephants, the
flanks by the cavalry.   Scipio formed his triple
line of maniples in columns of cohorts.   This
formation, which at Cannæ had proved vicious
in face of a superior cavalry, was well suited to
meet the charge of the elephants.   It left wide
avenues through the ranks, down which the huge
beasts might be drawn or driven by the skirmishers who filled the intervals.   Lælius commanded the Italian troopers on the left wing,
and Massinissa the Numidian light horse on the
right.   Both generals addressed stirring appeals
to their soldiers.   Scipio told his troops that their
only safety lay in victory, a victory which would
make Rome mistress of the world.   Hannibal had
a special word for every section of his motley
army.   To the foreigners, whether Spaniards
Celts or Macedonians, the last relics of the
great league he had planned, he spoke of pay
and plunder; the Carthaginians he bade re-
member wives and children, hearth and home;
his Italian veterans were reminded of the great
days of Trasimene and Cannæ.

Battle of   Hannibal opened the battle with a charge of
Zama.   elephants.   But the ponderous and imposing line
soon broke in wild confusion.   The beasts, raw
and untrained, were scared by the blast of the

npets, and harassed by a shower of
m the light troops. Some passed
lown the openings between Scipio's
ers, turning to right or left, threw the
· into disorder. With prompt decision
d Lælius seized their opportunity, and
_ _ _ discomfited horsemen, drove them in
full flight from the field. In the centre the struggle
was long and stern. For a time the agility and
daring of the mercenaries gave them the advantage
over the Roman *Hastati*. But the deafening cheers
of the legionaries, overpowering the dissonant
cries that broke from every part of the motley
crowd opposed to them, sounded the note of
victory. Once more the Roman spear and sword
proved superior to the Celtic claymore and the
Macedonian pike; once more discipline triumphed
over savage valour. The *Hastati*, sustained by the
steady support of the second line, forced the mercenaries back. The infuriated barbarians, when
they found themselves left unsupported by the
wavering civic militia, raised the cry of treachery,
and turned their arms against their hated and
distrusted masters. In the frenzied struggle, both
divisions were thrown back on Hannibal's Italian
reserve, while Scipio's first line also fell into confusion. At this point there would seem to have
been a short lull in the battle. Scipio, who should
have ordered an immediate advance, paused to
reform his troops. In the centre he gathered

together the remnants of his *Hastati*, while he deployed his second and third divisions in a single line on the right and left. Hannibal used the respite given him to withdraw his broken troops to the flanks and to push forward his Italian reserves. Then came the last fierce struggle between the desperate valour of Hannibal's veterans and the dogged obstinacy of the Roman legions. While the issue was still doubtful, Massinissa and Lælius returned at length from their hot pursuit of the beaten cavalry, and fell in force upon the Punic rear. The outnumbered and surrounded remnant, like the Old Guard at Waterloo, preferred death to surrender. When all was lost, Hannibal fled with a handful of his men to Hadrumetum.

Hannibal makes Peace, 201 B.C. Further resistance was out of the question, especially as the arrival of a fleet under P. Lentulus and the rout of Vermina's Numidian cavalry enabled Scipio to threaten Carthage both by sea and land. Hannibal was entrusted with the conduct of the negotiations, and secured for his vanquished country terms which were just if not generous. The surrender of all prisoners and deserters, a fine of 25,000 lbs. of silver in compensation for the plundered convoy, with the cession of all dominions abroad, were conditions which must have been foreseen. But the burning of the navy and its permanent reduction to ten vessels, the surrender of all elephants, the imposition of a war indemnity of two hundred talents a year for

...rs, guaranteed by hostages, and the
·t Carthage should not without
.nake war outside its own territories,
.1early that Carthage was now a tributary
at the mercy of Rome. To rivet her
·ins Massinissa was set beside her, a ready tool
..1 the hands of the suzerain power; while in case
this friend and ally of Rome should grow too
strong, his rival Vermina was left a part of his
father's ancient kingdom. Roman policy loved
this complicated system of checks and balances,
and was content to maim instead of slaying its
enemies. The political power of Carthage was
annihilated; was it necessary, as Cato thought, to
destroy an ancient seat of commerce, agriculture
and civilisation? No doubt the fear of a defence
animated by despair and conducted by the genius
of Hannibal helped to prevent Scipio from pushing Carthage to extremities, but we need not deny
to the Roman the far-sighted statesmanship and
noble generosity which refrained from a furious
and extravagant vengeance, nor to Hannibal a
magnanimous submission to the inevitable. He
did not even now forego his hopes of revenge, but
he knew that a defeated nation must husband its
resources, and patiently await the turning of fortune's wheel. With his own hand he had dragged
down from the rostrum a foolish agitator who had
dared to declaim against the peace, and with a curt
apology for his ignorance of the customs of civil

life, had silenced futher opposition, well knowing
that the renewal of war spelled ruin. He now
firmly repressed the mourning at Carthage for the
destruction of the fleet, and mocked with a bitter
laugh the rich Senators, who first began to bewail
the degradation of their country when called on
to contribute towards the war indemnity.

Rome and Italy.

Rome had been filled with alarm when first
it became known that Hannibal had assembled
in Africa a powerful army, which might well
destroy Scipio's weaker force. Anxiety gave place
to exultation at the glad tidings of victory and
peace. Scipio returned in triumph, saluted by
his soldiers conqueror of Africa (*Africanus*), and
welcomed by his native land and city as their
deliverer. Rome could now mete out rewards
and punishments at her leisure. Heavy as had
been the doom of Capua, a worse fate befell the
Bruttians, henceforth the serfs and bondsmen of
Rome. Dearly did the allies of Hannibal pay for
their offence in confiscations and executions, in
forfeiture of lands and liberties. The defeat of the
Carthaginian led to a second subjugation of Italy,
in which the hand of the victor fell heavily on the
alien races, the Gauls the Greeks the Etruscans
and the Sabellians, while it exalted her loyal
friends and kinsmen of the Latin name.

Character of the War.

If the solid fruits of victory fell to Rome, the
honours of the war remained with Hannibal. All
inprovements in strategy and tactics were first

taught by him, and afterwards painfully learned
by his Roman pupils. In the early years of the
war his lessons had been enforced by a series of
triumphs; then came a long and terrible struggle,
in which the Roman generals only escaped
disaster by a caution which verged on timidity;
at last Nero and Scipio profited by his example
to introduce a freer system of tactics and a
bolder strategy. Yet they but turned against
the Carthaginian the arms he himself had forged.
The use of a central position had been repeatedly
shown by Hannibal when Nero made that great
march to the Metaurus, which remained unequalled till Marlborough crossed half Europe to
win Blenheim. The battle of Zama was won for
Scipio by that Numidian cavalry which had
more than once proved itself the deadliest weapon
in Hannibal's armoury. No single man could
justly claim the credit for the defeat of Hannibal.
In the breadth of his combinations and the
subtlety of his tactics he far excelled the greatest
of his opponents; more than once he threatened
the very life of Rome. But in the end the stern
self-sacrifice and steadfast resolution of a nation
conquered the genius of an individual. Deserted
by his allies, unsupported by his country, Hannibal found his strength worn down by the firm
resistance of Latin Italy. Undefeated and undis-
mayed, he yet found himself isolated in a corner
of the land he came to conquer, and at last

Compelled to return home and stake all on the hazard of a doubtful battle. One curious feature of the war remains to be noticed, the absence of important naval operations. On the whole, Rome kept the command of the sea, wrested from Carthage in the earlier war, yet Mago could pass unopposed from Spain to Genoa, and Hannibal from Croton to Africa. Plainly the energies of Carthage were diverted from naval to military service, while Rome saw the necessity of maintaining communication with Spain and preventing an invasion of Italy. Yet it may be doubted if a command of the sea, such as Nelson established against Napoleon, was possible with the unseaworthy vessels of antiquity. As no efficient blockade could be maintained, the navies and convoys of both sides sailed freely over the waters. Rome as usual secured the one point of vital importance; Carthage left hundreds of ships unemployed in her dockyards to become the prey of the conqueror.

Results of the War.

The Hannibalic war settled the destiny of the western world. It was not only that Rome had acquired new provinces in Spain and Eastern Sicily, but also that she had formed relations in Africa and with the Hellenistic kingdoms of the East, which must inevitably lead to further conquest. She had striven only to win and to hold a secure sovereignty over Italy, but in so doing she had quite unconsciously taken the path to

Empire. Retreat was impossible; step by step Rome was pushed forward till her sway extended over every country in the civilised world. Nor was the spread of her dominion the gravest problem Rome had to face. In the war, the number of the citizens had fallen by a fourth; 300,000 Italians, the flower of the nation, had perished; trade commerce and agriculture had been shaken to their foundations. The class of yeomen, wasted by war and demoralised by camp life, dwindled away before the encroachments of large landowners, whose estates were worked by slaves. The dispossessed husbandmen sought occupation as professional soldiers, or flocked to swell the idle and dangerous mob of the capital. The corroding influence of social disintegration, and the imperious requirements of foreign dominion, undermined the republican constitution. In the end Rome must sacrifice liberty, that a Cæsar might give the world peace order and unity.

Yet we may not quarrel with the decrees of Fate. It is idle to speculate what new civilisation might have bloomed, had the Mediterranean continued to be the highway of independent peoples, bordered by a free Carthage, a revived Hellas, a new-born Syria. The existence side by side of separate nations in mutual tolerance, if not in amity, is a modern ideal foreign to the sentiments of antiquity. 'In ancient times it was necessary to be either anvil or hammer;' and in the great duel of the Punic wars, victory remained with the worthier combatant. A Punic empire could never have done for the world that which the rule of Rome accomplished. Carthage could not have absorbed the civilisation of Greece, or have trans-mitted it to the ruder races of the West and North: she could not have softened racial antipathies by the spread of a common literature and language; least of all could she have founded that great system of law which bound together barbarians of every race and tongue, and fitted them to become members of the great commonwealth of modern Europe.

CHAPTER VIII

THE LAST YEARS OF HANNIBAL

FOR fifty years after the battle of Zama, Rome *Roman* had a career of continuous conquest. The tramp *Conquest of the* of the legions is heard in every country, as, borne *West.* forward by fate, the Romans, like the English in India, first protect and then annex the decaying States around them, by right of their strong arm and genuine instinct for government. The Gauls, too late, resisted the steady advance of Rome towards the Alps. Under a Punic officer left behind by Mago, they sacked Placentia and besieged Cremona, but (200 B.C.) the Carthaginian was slain, and the town relieved. Nevertheless, the Boii and Insubres defended themselves with savage valour, till at length the discipline of the legions proved too strong for the fickle and divided clans. Gaul south of the Po was rapidly Latinised, while north of the river the Insubres and Cenomani were left to serve as bulwarks against the inroads of their Transalpine kinsmen. The Ligurians, cooped up in their rocky fastnesses, long maintained a guerrilla warfare ; but the frequent forays never rose to the dignity of a serious struggle.

In Spain, Rome ruled over the richer and more settled districts on the southern and eastern coasts, where Greeks and Phœnicians had already founded cities, and taught the natives mining, agriculture and other arts; but in the mountainous regions of Central and North-western Spain, barbarous tribes held fast to the rude liberty enjoyed by their ancestors. Rome made way but slowly in this rugged country, for the tribesmen fought fiercely in the field, and died heroically in defence of their walls. The work of conquest first accomplished by Cato (195 B.C.) needed to be done again and again. Sometimes the skill and courage of a warrior chieftain, more often the incompetence of Roman generals, led the legions to destruction, but the Spanish hosts, like the Highland armies of Montrose and Dundee, were too loosely bound together, and too impatient of discipline, to survive defeat or to follow up a victory. The surprises and massacres which mark the course of a predatory and irregular warfare give a stamp of treachery and cruelty to this objectless but unceasing conflict.

Roman Intervention in the East. If we turn our eyes eastward, we see Rome profiting by the dissensions which prevented all concert between the severed members of Alexander's mighty empire, to secure for herself the lion's share of the spoil. Nevertheless throughout she played the easy part of protecting quiet and pacific states against the turbulent aggression of

ambitious monarchs. With Macedon, Rome herself had good grounds of quarrel. The Senate
had neither forgotten nor forgiven Philip's alliance
with Hannibal after Cannæ, and the presence of
a Macedonian contingent at Zama. When the
king sought compensation for his failure in the
West by a savage attack on the coasts and islands
of Thrace and Asia Minor, he provoked a rupture.
Though weary of war, the reluctant people was
driven to arms by the determination of the Senate.
Philip, whose treachery and cruelty had embittered
his enemies and alienated his friends, was left to
bear the brunt of the Roman attack alone. Yet
he defended himself for three years with vigour
and success, till on the field of Cynoscephalæ,
the mobile and flexible legions triumphed over
the ponderous and unwieldy phalanx (197 B.C.).
Philip, reduced to the rank of a vassal, was
allowed to retain his hereditary kingdom, while
Greece received from Flamininus the doubtful
boon of liberty (196 B.C.).

While Rome thus moved forward from conquest Hannibal
to conquest, Carthage had to tread the stony path as a States-
of humiliation and dishonour. Massinissa, as had man.
been designed by the Senate, proved a constant
thorn in her side, nor were appeals to the suzerain
of any avail. With true Oriental patience she
turned her cheek to the smiter, waiting in vain for
a day of reckoning. Hannibal, beaten in war by
a cruel fate, now undertook the hardest tasks of

statesmanship, to reform a rotten government and
to revive the spirit of a beaten nation. The Punic
oligarchy had filled up the cup of its iniquities
by bringing against him the impudent accusations that he had purposely spared Rome and
embezzled the plunder of Italy. Called to the
office of Shofete by the patriot party, Hannibal
overthrew the oligarchy by striking at the narrow
and exclusive board of the hundred judges (195
B.C.). Whatever may have been the theory of the
constitution, in practice the judges were chosen by
favour, and held office for long periods. Hannibal
substituted free annual election, and thus established democracy at Carthage. He also reformed
the financial system, and by collecting arrears and
compelling corrupt officials to disgorge their ill-
gotten gains, provided for the payment of the sum
due annually to Rome without imposing additional taxes. So effective was his re-organisation
that within ten years (187 B.C.) his successors
were ready to pay off the whole remainder of the
war indemnity. Embittered by the loss of power
and gain, the selfish nobility denounced Hannibal
for communicating secretly with the enemies of
Rome. The Senate, which viewed with apprehen-
sion the approaching struggle with Antiochus of
Syria, despatched an embassy to Carthage to
demand the surrender of Hannibal. It was a
humiliating confession that Rome lived in terror
of a single man. Yet it was the simple truth that

Hannibal, and not Carthage, had fought the last war, and was the true enemy to be feared in the future. Hannibal spared his countrymen the crowning disgrace of complying with the Roman demand by a speedy and secret flight. Carthage was compelled to banish her greatest citizen, to confiscate his goods and raze his house to the ground (195 B.C.).

Hannibal sought refuge with Antiochus at Ephesus, and was at first received with the highest honours. But it was his fate once more to be baffled by the perversity of the master he strove to serve. In vain he begged for a small fleet and army, with which he undertook to renew the war in Africa, and thence descend on Italy as the forerunner of the Eastern hosts. Meanwhile, the Syrian king was to advance by land, drawing support as he went from Greece and Macedon, from Gauls and Ligurians, and to join hands with Hannibal in Italy. But Antiochus, misnamed the Great by Oriental flattery, had not the mind to comprehend this grand scheme, nor the magnanimity to submit his judgment to that of the illustrious exile. Pluming himself on his independence, the 'great' king was induced by a petty court cabal to reject Hannibal's counsels, and to relegate him to inferior commands. Carthage unaided had no course open but instant submission; Philip of Macedon had not forgiven the neutrality of the faithless Syrian during his late war with

Hannibal and Antiochus.

Rome; only the restless Ætolians were zealous for
the king's cause. Antiochus landed in Greece, to be
ignominiously routed at Thermopylæ, and driven
headlong back to Ephesus (191 B.C.). Hannibal,
whose advice was scornfully disregarded, followed,
a helpless spectator in the wake of the Syrian
army. At last Antiochus found employment for
the greatest soldier of the day by sending him to
sea, commissioned to bring up a Phœnician fleet·
In an engagement off Aspendus, Hannibal, in
spite of superior tactics, was defeated by the skill
and valour of Rome's Rhodian sailors, though by
directing his retreat towards the shore he preserved his squadron from disaster. It was his
first naval battle, and his last encounter with his
lifelong foes.

Battle of
Magnesia. Hannibal returned to Ephesus to find that the
Roman legions under the Scipios had crossed to
Asia. Near Magnesia, in the valley of the Hermus,
Antiochus had gathered together from his wide
empire a typical Eastern host. The Syrian army
numbered some 60,000 foot and 12,000 horse, with
54 elephants; the Roman, including 5000 Greek
auxiliaries, only 30,000 men. Yet, when the king
asked Hannibal whether he did not think his
forces enough for the Romans, the Carthaginian
answered grimly,—

'Oh, yes, enough for the Romans, greedy as
they are.' He foresaw that the small but disciplined Western army would easily overthrow the

glittering multitudes of the East. The Roman left rested on the river, covered only by four squadrons of horse, the legions held the centre, while the bulk of the cavalry and all the light troops were massed on the right wing, under Eumenes of Pergamum. Antiochus drew up his phalanx in ten solid squares, each with a front of fifty and a depth of thirty-two file, posting his elephants on the flanks and in the intervals of this imposing but unwieldy mass. On either side the phalanx were Gallic and Cappadocian infantry, while thousands of cuirassiers and dragoons, supported by a number of light troops, formed the wings of the Syrian army. In front of his left the king stationed a camel corps, some mounted archers, and a useless row of scythed chariots. Eumenes began the battle by sending his archers and slingers against the chariots, with orders to shoot down the teams, and thus fling chariots and camel corps in helpless confusion back upon the second line. Seizing the favourable moment, he charged the cuirassiers with all his cavalry, and after routing the whole left wing of the Syrians, threatened the flank of the phalanx. Meanwhile, Antiochus had swept away the few squadrons of horse opposed to him, but had been baffled in an assault on the Roman camp by the vigorous resistance of its garrison. As he turned back to the battle he beheld his army in full retreat. The phalanx, though its solid masses were decimated by a storm of missiles from all sides, retired slowly and in good order, until the frightened elephants broke up its ranks. Then came a general flight and hideous massacre. The conquest of Asia cost the Romans nothing but the loss of a few allies (190 B.C.).

Death of Hannibal (183 B.C.). Rome assumed a protectorate over Asia Minor north of Mount Taurus, compelling Antiochus to resign an empire too large, as he jestingly said, for one man to govern. Among the conditions of an ignominious peace was the surrender of Hannibal. But the Carthaginian again fled, and wandered about a homeless fugitive. Probably Scipio, who had already protested against his expulsion from Carthage, did not care to hunt down his unfortunate antagonist. We hear of Hannibal in Crete and in Armenia; at last he found a refuge at the court of Prusias, King of Bithynia. Oriental legend makes Hannibal, like Alexander, a founder of cities—Prusa in Bithynia, and Artaxata, the capital of Armenia. History records that he aided Prusias in his wars with Eumenes of Pergamum. At length Flamininus, the liberator of Greece, undertook the task which Scipio had declined—the deliverance of Rome from all fear of Hannibal. Prusias, the most pitiful of all the pitiful princelings of Asia, readily granted the request of the Roman envoy, and betrayed his illustrious guest to his implacable foes. For the last time the Carthaginian baulked their malice, for seeing his house beset by assassins he took poison, and thus escaped the dungeon and the axe awaiting him at Rome. He had begun his career with a fair prospect of regaining for Carthage the empire of the Mediterranean, he had lived to see the West subdued and the East bow down almost without a struggle before the power of Rome. When he died in exile an old man at sixty-three, he had outlived all his hopes, and had nothing but dishonour left to fear.

By a strange coincidence, Scipio Africanus Death of passed away almost at the same time. All his Scipio. brilliant victories and all his high ideals ended in vanity and vexation of spirit. The charges of bribery and embezzlement, brought against him and his brother Lucius, were doubtless calumnies, prompted by dislike for his arrogant bearing and family policy. Characteristically enough, he would not stoop to prove his innocence by a commonplace appeal to account books, but tore them in pieces before his accusers and the people, calling on all true Romans to follow him to the Capitol, and join in celebrating the anniversary of Zama. Yet in spite of a momentary burst of enthusiasm, Lucius Scipio was fined, and Publius withdrew from Rome to eat his heart in exile. With his last breath he reproached his native city with ingratitude, and refused to be buried there, in the tomb of his fathers.

Compari-
son of
Hannibal
with Alex-
ander,
Cæsar and
Napoleon
as a
States-
man.

It is not, however, with such a man as Scipio Africanus, whose character is a curious mixture of true gold and glittering tinsel, that Hannibal should be compared. To find his peers we must look among the heroes of all time, the master spirits whose greatness can finally be weighed only in the balances of God. He may be set beside Alexander, Cæsar and Napoleon. It might be argued that his genius has not, like theirs, changed the face of the civilised world. Alexander's empire fell to pieces at his death, but his greater work was not undone, though left unfinished. His type of colonisation, his principles of provincial government, his standard of currency, and his military system prevailed in the East until the coming of Rome. More than any other man, too, he broke down the barrier between Greek and barbarian, and thus paved the way for a universal empire and a catholic church. Cæsar, amidst the ruins of a worn-out civilisation, founded a new harmonious and enduring order, which conferred on mankind the priceless blessings of law peace and unity. Napoleon, if never destined to realise all his grand dreams of conquest, yet destroyed feudalism in Western Europe, and created all that is best and most stable in the institutions of France. Hannibal alone seems to have left behind him no work that has stood the test of time. Yet even as a statesman and patriot he ranks with the immortals. If he failed, the fault lay not with the reformer who strove to enkindle with his own ardour a defeated and dispirited nation, nor with the statesman who devised the great league that should have crushed Rome; it is to be found in the despicable weakness of the Punic oligarchy and the blind inconstancy of the Macedonian king. And in one point at least he stands above his peers. Selfish ambition mingles with loftier motives in the magnificent schemes of Alexander, of Napoleon, and even of Cæsar, but in Hannibal there is nothing save the one consuming passion of patriotism, of which he was in life the pattern, and in death the martyr.

In war, the special sphere of his genius, Comparison of Hannibal with these great Captains in War. Hannibal remains unsurpassed. Other great captains have indeed excelled him in particular branches of the military art. Alexander showed a swiftness both in his first attack and in the pursuit of a beaten enemy never equalled by Hannibal. Alexander at Tyre, and Cæsar at Alesia, displayed in the conduct of sieges a skill and persistency conspicuously absent from the similar operations of the Carthaginian. Napoleon at times conceived ideas and schemes of a yet more dazzling brilliance, but the sanguine and impetuous emperor had not the coolness and the tenacity of Hannibal. Indeed, if we take into account all the disadvantages under which Hannibal laboured, his superiority is evident. Alexander led his father's veterans against a disorderly rabble of Orientals; Napoleon could draw without stint on the resources in men and money of an empire; even Cæsar never faced an army superior in numbers and equal in valour and training to his veterans; Hannibal, on the other hand, had to contend with enemies of six times his own strength, not inferior in arms discipline or courage to his own troops, and yet brought Rome to the verge of ruin. He may justly be called the father of strategy, capable alike of the boldest designs, such as his march over the Alps, and of the most prudent self-restraint, as in his decision not to advance on Rome after Cannæ. He always brought his forces to bear on the most decisive points in the field of operations, while by constantly taking the initiative, and hiding his purpose till the last moment, he found frequent opportunities of assailing his disconcerted adversaries in flank and rear. Less venturesome than Napoleon and Alexander, he was deeper and more subtle. As a tactician, Hannibal has no superior, perhaps no equal. He wins his battles by taking full advantage of the nature of the ground, by determined blows at the most vulnerable points in the enemy's forces and position, and by the free use of his strongest arm, cavalry. His crowning excellences were the studied variety of his tactics, and his wonderful skill in ambushes and stratagems. Alexander may have been a greater leader of cavalry, but the son of Philip disdained to steal a victory, and too often in the heat of battle would fight like a paladin rather than guide and control as a general. Hannibal, under all circumstances, remained cool and resourceful, self-reliant and self-restrained. Nor is he inferior to the other great captains in ascendency over the generals opposed to him, and the troops under his command. Alexander Cæsar and Napoleon were dreaded by their opponents and worshipped by their followers. But they led men of their own blood to battle with foes whom they were accustomed to vanquish. Hannibal faced a victorious nation at the head of an army of many races and many tongues, yet that army followed him without a murmur for seventeen years, and fought for him to the death when all hope was gone.

By the irony of fate the work of this great hero perished before his eyes. Even for the record of his achievements and of his character we depend in the main on the descriptions of enemies who neither understood nor cared to understand his real greatness. Of his private life and conversation we know little or nothing. His epitaph on Marcellus, 'There lies a good soldier but a bad general,' and his brief comment on the Ephesian sophist who discoursed for hours before him on

Hannibal's Greatness.

the duties of a general, 'Many dotards have I met, but never one so mad as this,' show the grim contempt of the real master of war for empty theory and for stubborn, unreasoning courage. Yet if we would judge Hannibal aright, we must look beyond the few pithy sayings preserved to us, and beyond the visible and tangible results of his unwearied activity to the ineffaceable impression made by his genius on the victors, and through their unwilling testimony on after ages. Rome might conquer and deserve to conquer, but it is the figure of Hannibal which rivets all eyes and stands forth from the pages of history. In that dread form the Romans saw a destroying angel having a drawn sword in his hand stretched out over Italy. Later ages have seen in him a hero of unstained patriotism and of unmatched military genius, great alike in his countless victories and in his one defeat. It surely adds to the pathos of his life that, with all his gifts and with all his zeal, he could not avenge his country of her enemies nor save her from humiliation and destruction.

INDEX

THE END

Lightning Source UK Ltd.
Milton Keynes UK
18 June 2010

155772UK00006BA/7/P